Hitler and the Jews

Hitler and the Jews

The Genesis of the Holocaust

Philippe Burrin

Professor of International History, The Graduate Institute
of International Studies, Geneva, Switzerland

Translated by Patsy Southgate

Introduction by Saul Friedländer

Edward Arnold
A member of the Hodder Headline Group
LONDON MELBOURNE AUCKLAND

© Editions du Seuil, 1989

First published in Great Britain 1994
First published under the title *Hitler et les Juifs: Genèse d'un génocide*
English translation © 1994 Patsy Southgate
Introduction to the English Edition © 1994 by Saul Friedländer

Distributed in the USA by Routledge, Chapman and Hall, Inc.
29 West 35th Street, New York, NY 10001

British Library Cataloguing in Publication Data

Burrin, Philippe
  Hitler and the Jews: The Genesis of the Holocaust
  I. Title
  940.5318

  ISBN 0-340-59361-X
      0-340-59362-8 pbk

Library of Congress Cataloguing-in-Publication Data

Burrin, Philippe, 1952–
  [Hitler et les Juifs, English]
  Hitler and the Jews : the genesis of the Holocaust / Philippe
Burrin : translated by Patsy Southgate : introduction by Saul
Friedländer.
    p.   cm.
  Includes bibliographical references and index.
  ISBN 0-340-59361-X : $59.95. -- ISBN 0-340-59362-8
(pbk.) : $16.95
  1. Holocaust, Jewish (1939–1945)--Causes. 2. Germany-
-Politics and government--1933–1945. 3. Hitler, Adolf,
1889–1945. I. Title. D804.3.B8713   1994
940.53'18--dc20   93–34024
                                                    CIP

Typeset in 11/12pt Palatino by Hewer Text Composition
Services, Edinburgh
Printed and bound in Great Britain for Edward Arnold, a
division of Hodder Headline PLC, Mill Road, Dunton Green,
Sevenoaks, Kent TN13 2YA by Biddles Ltd, Guildford and
King's Lynn

To Saul Friedländer

Contents

Acknowledgements   ix
Introduction to the English Edition *Saul Friedländer*   1
Introduction   17
1.   Hitler's Anti-Semitism   25
2.   The Emigration Policy, 1933–1939   41
3.   The Quest for a Territorial Solution, 1939–1941   65
4.   The Fate of the Soviet Jews   93
5.   The Final Decision   115
6.   Hitler and the Genocide   133
7.   Conclusion   149
Notes   155
Index   175

Acknowledgements

My thanks go to the heads of the various archival centres I had occasion to frequent during the preparation of this work, notably to Alfred Streim and Willi Dressen (Ludwigsburg). I would like to express particular gratitude to Sarah Halperyn and Widar Jacobsen of the Centre for Contemporary Jewish Documentation; I have benefited over the years from their friendly and competent assistance.

Introduction to the English Edition*

Saul Friedländer

Can a person to whom a book has been dedicated write its introduction? The answer, I think, is simple: any introduction aims at presenting a book in favourable terms, whatever the evaluation of specific issues may be. It need not shy away from raising questions, and I shall not do so here. However, the decisive fact for me was that Philippe Burrin's book constitutes, to my mind, a remarkable contribution to the history of the extermination of the Jews of Europe, in terms of his use of new material, the coherence of his analysis, and the originality of his interpretations.

I shall first refer very briefly to Burrin's interpretation of Hitler's ideology and of Nazi policies towards the Jews in the 1930s, as well as at the beginning of the war, until the German attack on the Soviet Union in June 1941. I shall then address the author's detailed analysis of the events of the summer and autumn of 1941 and consider some of the central questions raised by his arguments. Finally, I shall briefly turn to the wider historiographical issues relating to the genesis of the Final Solution.

I

In his introduction, Burrin clearly summarizes the existing approaches to the Nazi policies towards the Jews, as these approaches have developed over the past three decades. It is unnecessary to review here the by now well-known

* I wish to thank Dr Dina Porat for her careful reading of this text and for her valuable suggestions.

diverging positions: those grounded in the primacy of intention and planning and those stressing an interaction of
unplanned moves and circumstances. Burrin opts for a
synthesis: 'Like the intentionalists, I believe that Hitler
harboured the intention of exterminating the Jews; this
intention, however, was not absolute, but conditional: it
would be carried out only in the event of a well-defined
situation. . . . Like the functionalists, on the other hand, I
maintain that a combination of circumstances was essential
to the fulfilment of this intention, for its translation into
action . . .'.

From the outset, therefore, Burrin's position concerning
Hitler's role and the decisive aspect of his anti-Semitism is
clear. Burrin sums up the main aspects of Hitler's anti-Jewish
ideology and highlights the central point of his overall argument: the traumatic effect of the German defeat in 1918, a
defeat caused, according to Hitler, by the Jews. This was
the event which turned Hitler's anti-Semitism into a 'central
obsession'. From that moment, Hitler's hatred of the Jews
assumed an absolutely cardinal place in his world-view: it
had become, above and beyond the widespread anti-Jewish
stances, his way of interpreting Germany's defeat in the war.
The Jews were the universal enemy which had relentlessly
led the external and internal war against Germany.

Burrin's basic thesis is that, at any sign of an all-out war
such as that of 1914–18, Hitler was prepared to direct his
fury against the Jews. In Burrin's view, Hitler had taken
his decision even before reaching power: if his projects
were to fail, the radical struggle against the Jews would
become paramount. There would be no new revolution or
capitulation as in 1918, and the Jews would pay dearly for
any obstacle in his path to domination. No new sign of
defeat would appear without a horrifying price being paid
by the Jews. This became the background to the decision for
extermination taken in the autumn of 1941.

During the 1920s, and no less so after the accession of the
Nazis to power, Hitler and the party hesitated about the precise ways of handling the 'Jewish question'. As we know, the
overall thrust of Nazi policy, from 1933 on, was the exclusion
of the Jews from German society and their expulsion from
the territory of the German Reich. That this policy followed
a 'twisted road'[1] is undeniable; that within six years it had
none the less achieved most of its aims is no less evident.

During this period Hitler apparently never lost sight of possible negative contingencies and their consequences for the Jews. On 25 September 1935, according to a document discovered by Burrin, Walter Gross, the head of the Racial Policy Office of the party, briefed the regional chiefs of his service about a conversation he had just had with Hitler regarding the 'Jewish question'. The party's aims remained the limitation of Jewish influence within Germany and the separation of the Jews from the body of the nation; the ultimate aim was their expulsion from Germany. Economic measures would be the next stage, but the party must not create a situation which would turn the Jews into a public burden; carefully calculated steps were needed. As for the Jews of mixed marriages, Hitler favoured their assimilation, within a few generations, in order to avoid any weakening of the German potential for war. A final and crucial point remained. According to the Gross protocol, Hitler declared that, in the case of a 'war on all fronts [*i.e. similar to the First World War*] . . . he would be ready for all the consequences [*as far as the Jews were concerned*]' ('An dieser Stelle, erkläet er noch, dass er im Falle eines Krieges auf allen Fronten "bereit zu allen Konsequenzen" sei').

Hitler's notorious speech to the Reichstag on 30 January 1939 was entirely in line with this obsession: if international Jewry within and outside Europe were again to push the peoples into a world war, the result would not be the Bolshevization of the earth and the victory of the Jews, but the annihilation of the Jewish race in Europe.

A few moments before uttering these threats, Hitler had declared that Europe would have no rest until the 'Jewish question' – a problem for the whole of Europe – was solved; he alluded to sufficient areas for colonization, where the Jews would have to work and stop being parasites. Thus, in Burrin's words, Hitler's 'threat of extermination was conditional: it would be carried out in the event of a world war, i.e. in a situation that meant the endangering . . . of his plan'.

As long as the war launched by Hitler in September 1939 led to a series of stunning victories for Germany, the Nazis continued searching for the 'territorial solution' to the Jewish question to which Hitler alluded in his January 1939 speech. The idea of a reservation around Lublin and the Madagascar project are their best-known plans. Expulsion eastward, deep into Russian territory, appeared as a solution once the preparations for the attack on the Soviet Union took shape. According to Burrin, this possibility remained under consideration even after the attack on the Soviet Union began on 22 June 1941, as long as the Germans hoped that Russia would collapse within a few weeks. At this point, however, we have reached the heart of Burrin's study and the major historical issues it raises.

II

According to Burrin, the exterminations perpetrated by the Einsatzgruppen on Soviet territory were not part of a general order for the Final Solution, and they developed incrementally; the order for the total extermination of the Jews of Europe was not given by Hitler before the attack on the Soviet Union or immediately afterwards, during the euphoria of initial victories, but in the autumn of 1941 (specifically, September), when doubts started growing about the progress of the campaign. I shall consider first the activities of the Einsatzgruppen, then the possible date of the order of total extermination, and, finally, the context of this order.

The interpretation of the murderous activities of the Einsatzgruppen from the beginning of the Russian campaign to early or mid-August 1941 has generated serious controversy. Some historians – in particular the German historian Helmut Krausnick[2] – maintain that an order to kill the entire Jewish population on Soviet territory was given to the Einsatzgruppen just before the outset of the campaign, and that their killings were, from the start, indiscriminately aimed at that entire population. Others, such as the German historian Alfred Streim,[3] assert that no such general order was given before the beginning of the attack on the Soviet Union, and that the murderous activities of the Einsatzgruppen were incremental, their scope expanding from early July. Burrin has adopted the second interpretation, in terms both of the orders given and of the scope of the killings.

As far as the written orders to the Einsatzgruppen are concerned, we know of only two documents containing references to the general instructions regarding the fate of the Jews in the newly conquered Soviet territory. The first is a letter from Heydrich of 2 July 1941, addressed to the higher SS and police chiefs, in which he sums up the orders given to the heads of the Einsatzgruppen: among other targets, all Jews in party and state positions should be executed and the Einsatzgruppen should encourage pogroms by the local populations. The second is a 17 July order from Heydrich that 'all Jews' among Russian prisoners of war should be executed. Much of the evidence, however, is based on postwar testimonies.

According to the testimony given at Nuremberg by Otto Ohlendorf, head of Einsatzgruppe D (the only head of an Einsatzgruppe put on trial), an oral order to exterminate all Jews on Soviet territory was transmitted by Bruno Streckenbach, an emissary from Heydrich, to the commanders of the Einsatzgruppen a few days before the beginning of the campaign. At the time of this testimony (1947), Streckenbach was thought to be dead. However, when he returned from a Russian prisoner-of-war camp in the mid-1950s, he declared that no such order was ever given or transmitted before the beginning of the Russian campaign. Other members of the killing units (heads or members of Einsatzkommandos, subunits of the Einsatzgruppen) who were put on trial were more or less equally divided in the support of either one of these opposing claims; moreover, any number of other versions which could help their defence were produced. Burrin offers a very thorough analysis of all the available testimonies and reaches the conclusion that, on the basis of this material, it would seem that no order for the overall extermination of Soviet Jews was given before or at the very outset of the campaign.

Burrin's argument is not based only on his analysis of the testimonies given at the trials of Einsatzgruppen members; he also looks for major evidence in the reports of the Einsatzgruppen for the period July–September 1941. At this point, two general remarks seem necessary.

As far as the sources are concerned, we not only possess the German documents about the activities of the Einsatzgruppen; we have significant evidence from Jewish sources too. There is a third source, however, soon to become accessible but not yet utilized: the Soviet documents. From 1943 on, a Soviet historical commission collected material about the German killings of civilians in occupied Soviet territory. Only after these three major sources are considered together will it be possible for a more or less complete picture to appear. Burrin relies essentially on German sources. As we shall see, Jewish sources seem to confirm his interpretation of the German material; what the Soviet material will reveal is still unknown.

Second, whatever the overall picture given by the reports about the Einsatzgruppen activities, there is no necessary correlation between this picture and the initial orders given to the killing units. There may have been an initial order for overall extermination of Jews on Soviet territory, although for several weeks the killings were directed mostly at men. As we shall see, this possibility, which is not perceived by Burrin, has been cogently argued.

Turning to the available material, one may, on the one hand, find the scale of the massacres perpetrated by Einsatzgruppen and local militias immediately after the invasion of the Soviet Union, especially in the Baltic countries, to be indicative of entirely new plans. There is a radical difference between the crimes committed by the Einsatzgruppen after the invasion of Poland and those committed after the invasion of the Soviet Union. On the other hand, one may also consider the reports of various Einsatzgruppen over a period of several weeks: these show a step-by-step progression in the killings, with a sharp increase in numbers leading toward the general extermination of the Jewish population on Soviet territory *by the beginning or middle of August 1941*. Burrin's analysis of these reports, in terms of their wording as well as with reference to the horrendous statistical breakdowns they offer, strongly points to the fact that during the first weeks of the campaign the killings were selective and the victims mostly men. Women and children were massively included in the overall massacre only from early or mid-August, as if a change of policy had taken place.[4] For instance, the day-by-day execution reports for June–December 1941, prepared by Karl Jäger, head of Einsatzkommando 3 of Einsatzgruppe A, indicate (according to Burrin) the following progression. In July, 4,239 Jews were murdered, 135 of whom were women. In August, the total number rose to 37,186, of whom 32,430 were killed after mid-August, massively including women and children. The 56,459 Jews killed in September comprised 15,104 men, 26,243 women, and 15,112 children.

One could argue that the reports (*Ereignismeldungen UdSSR*) of the Einsatzgruppen were only one aspect of a larger framework in which the killings were also perpetrated by German-directed local militias, by Waffen SS units, and, in the south, by units of the Romanian army probably instigated by the Germans. Burrin, however, takes into account research on both the local militias and Waffen SS units, albeit briefly.[5]

Burrin's assessment of the facts is confirmed by other major research. Christopher Browning's study, *Ordinary Men*, indicates that the units of the German 'Ordnungpolizei' who were involved in the killing of Jews on Soviet territory during July and early August were given orders mentioning the killing of Jewish men. For instance, the following order was issued to the Police Regiment Centre on 10 July: 'By order of the Higher SS and Police Leader . . . all male Jews between the ages of 17 and 45 convicted as plunderers are to be shot according to martial law. The shootings are to take place away from cities, villages, and thoroughfares.'[6] Similar orders appear during the next few weeks.

The most thorough study of the extermination of the Jews of Lithuania was published in 1976 by the Israeli historian Itzhak Arad. This study, based on German and Jewish sources as well, clearly confirms the fact that through the month of July 1941 the victims of the Einsatzgruppen in Lithuania were 'almost uniquely men'.[7] However, Arad, who believes that a general extermination order was given before the beginning of the campaign, offers a possible explanation of the almost exclusive killing of men in July and early August: killing the men first ensured that women and children could easily be killed later on, as, left to themselves, they had no means of defence or escape. Moreover, when the men were taken away, the SS assured the Jewish populations that they were being sent to distant work sites, an explanation which would not have been credible if women and children had been included. In fact, some of the men were sent to work and allowed to return to their homes.[8] We recognize a notorious pattern: the killers systematically attempted to deceive their victims, in order to avoid chaos and possible resistance. Support for a somewhat similar interpretation can be found in Richard Breitman's *The Architect of Genocide*:

> it is logical that Himmler and Heydrich gave *Einsatzgruppen* commanders instructions to eliminate the most dangerous enemies first, if they could not deal with everyone. So it is not really surprising that in some areas police units murdered Jewish men, women, and children from the very beginning, while in others they limited their killing to Jewish men, or,

even more narrowly, to Jewish intellectuals and potential leaders.[9]

Notwithstanding the uncertainty about the significance of the killings perpetrated by local militias within the overall German action, Burrin's interpretation seems to me plausible for one single reason: had the killing of men during the initial phase of the German campaign been a well-thought-through tactical step, applied by all the Einsatzgruppen in order quickly to entrap the whole Jewish population, or to deal with the most dangerous enemies first, mention of this tactic would have appeared in some German document. To my knowledge, no such explicit mention has been found.

If we follow Burrin's argumentation and assume that no order of general extermination of Soviet Jews was given before or at the outset of the Russian campaign, we have to accept the corollary that no order of an overall extermination of European Jewry was given before 22 June 1941, or soon after the beginning of the German attack. This leads us to the issue of the date on which the order for the Final Solution was possibly given.

Very schematically, the following positions have been presented regarding the genesis of the decision totally to exterminate European Jewry. Some historians argue that the decision not only had deep ideological foundations but was definitively taken *before* the attack on the Soviet Union. This position was most recently defended by Gerald Fleming and Richard Breitman.

A second approach argues that the extermination of all Soviet Jewry was decided before the attack against the Soviet Union, but that the decision for the overall extermination of the Jews was probably taken in the weeks immediately following the attack, during the period of euphoria when a quick Russian collapse was still regarded as highly probable by the Germans. This position has been most minutely and cogently presented by Christopher Browning.[10] According to Browning:

> The intention of systematically murdering the European Jews was not fixed in Hitler's mind before the war, but crystallized in 1941 after previous solutions proved unworkable and the imminent attack upon Russia raised the prospect of yet another vast increase in the number of Jews within the growing German empire. The 'Final Solution' emerged out of a series of decisions taken that year. In the spring Hitler

ordered preparations for the murder of the Russian Jews who would fall into German hands during the coming invasion. That summer, confident of military victory, Hitler instigated the preparation of a plan to extend the killing process to European Jews. In October, although military expectations had not been realized, Hitler approved the rough outline of that plan, involving deportation to killing centers using poison gas.[11]

The same events, differently interpreted, can be seen as indicating that the decision was taken in the autumn. This is the position held by Uwe Dietrich Adam, Eberhard Jäckel, and Burrin.[12] Finally, some historians, particularly Martin Broszat, Hans Mommsen, and, to a certain extent, Arno Mayer, have argued that no single decision was ever taken by Hitler – that the process was cumulative, and initiated by a series of measures by local SS authorities rather than by Berlin. No clear order was ever given by Hitler, nor, according to this view, was it necessary.[13]

Although for a long time I felt convinced by the first position,[14] I now tend to accept Burrin's argument. There was an order from Hitler for the total extermination of European Jewry, most probably issued in September of 1941. Burrin brings new documents to bolster his general argument. Other major evidence has to be accounted for.

On 31 July 1941, Heydrich received a general order from Goering to take all necessary measures in preparation for an all-encompassing solution to the Jewish question in the German-controlled areas of Europe. Many historians have considered this document as *the* order marking the beginning of the preparations for the overall extermination of European Jewry. Others – Burrin among them – referring *inter alia* to Eichmann's testimony on this matter – believe that the letter was the result of an initiative taken by Heydrich with the aim of acquiring control of all aspects of the solution to the 'Jewish question', on the assumption that the victory against the Soviet Union would open any number of possibilities for such a 'solution': general deportation, slave labour in the east or, possibly, mass murder. In subsequently referring to the Goering order, Heydrich indicated that it constituted the formal basis for the various measures he was taking to deal with the Jewish issue. Here, indeed, lay the basis of his authority over the co-ordination between state agencies and the SS, which was one of the main aims of the January 1942

Wannsee meeting. Within this general context Heydrich was told, probably in September 1941, that the policy would be that of total extermination.

Burrin's most important new documentary evidence, pointing to approximately mid-September as the date of the order for the general extermination of the Jews of Europe, is a Heydrich communication to the OKH (the High Command of the Army) on 6 November 1941. During the night of 2–3 October a group of French collaborators, led by Eugene Deloncle, set off explosives in several Paris synagogues. As it soon became clear that the action had been taken with Heydrich's consent, the Wehrmacht commander in France, Otto von Stuelpnagel, complained in Berlin about such independent initiatives. Heydrich's answer to the High Command of the Army was clear: he (Heydrich) had accepted the suggestion of the leader of the French group, 'only from the moment when, at the highest level, Jewry had been forcefully designated as the culpable incendiary in Europe, one which must definitively disappear from Europe' ('Seine Vorschläege wurden von mir erst in dem Augenblick angenommen, als auch von hoechster Stelle, mit aller Schäerfe, das Judentum als der verantwortliche Brandstifter in Europa gekennzeichnet wurde, der endgüeltig in Europe verschwinden muss'). As the attacks against the synagogues were perpetrated during the night of 2–3 October, Heydrich's words 'only from the moment when' could indicate a date in September.

Burrin does not base his argument on Heydrich's document only, but on a series of converging elements. On 4 October 1941, for instance, Heydrich discussed the Jewish question with Gauleiter Mayer, chief aide to Alfred Rosenberg, minister for the Eastern Territories since 17 July 1941. Heydrich raised the question whether the Rosenberg ministry should 'still' have its own delegates for Jewish affairs or whether this should not be left to the SS only. The word 'still' is obviously of the essence. Moreover, the document indicates that Heydrich was worried that various economic enterprises would insist on keeping their Jewish workers and had not taken measures to train alternative manpower; this could 'reduce to naught the plan for a total resettlement of the Jews out of the territories occupied by us'. As Burrin indicates, this document shows that those involved considered that they were at the beginning of a vast project and worried about possible obstacles. As for a total transfer plan in October

1941, it could mean only death, as the continuing war on the Soviet front left no option of new territories in the east.

Even more telling is a letter of 9 October from the SS commander of the Lodz region, Friedrich Übelhor, to Berlin, complaining that for a few days the Gestapo had been working at a reorganization of the Lodz ghetto: 40,000 Jews were to be transferred to a 'work ghetto' (*Arbeitsghetto*), whereas more than 100,000 Jews unable to work would be relocated in a 'maintenance ghetto' (*Versorgungsghetto*), the area of which was one-quarter that of the first one. For Uebelhoer, this was leading to an impossible situation. But the meaning of the Gestapo action was clear enough: the inhabitants of the *Versorgungsghetto* were to be exterminated. Indeed, at the end of October the extermination commando Lange arrived in Chelmno, in the vicinity of Lodz, and started preparing the extermination site.

The last two documents could also indicate the final stages of a plan whose preparation had started in July. However, when considered together with Heydrich's letter to the OKH, they bolster the hypothesis of a decision probably taken in September, the quick implementation of which was becoming apparent within a few weeks.

The third major issue raised by Burrin is the context of Hitler's decision. According to Burrin's overall thesis, the context was the prolongation of the Soviet campaign, which was turning the war into a situation similar to that of the First World War, with the possibility of another defeat. Such an outcome had to be avoided at all costs, first of all by the elimination of the most treacherous internal enemies, the Jews. This interpretation tallies with Hitler's statements in the 1920s and 1930s, with Walter Gross's report of 1935, and with the 'prophecy' Hitler made in his Reichstag speech of 30 January 1939.

However, the question is whether, by mid-September 1941, Hitler already foresaw a prolonged war and the danger of defeat. There is no document that unequivocally supports such a hypothesis. The numerous excerpts from Hitler's statements quoted by Burrin in the last chapter indicate a recurring mixture of doubts and euphoria, of fears and certainty about the outcome of the campaign, from approximately mid-July on. Nothing seems to distinguish the moods expressed in September from those of the previous months. In September, moreover, the Kiev battle was just ending with

the capture of a stupendous number of Russian prisoners
(over 600,000); operation Typhoon, aimed at the capture of
Moscow, was launched on 2 October. The delays in the initial
campaign plan had been apparent for several months, but
it was only in November that the stalling of Typhoon gave
a clear warning signal. How, then, should we consider the
context suggested by Burrin?

It seems that this context can be defined along the lines of
Burrin's interpretation, but in slightly different terms. At the
time of the attack on the Soviet Union, Hitler announced on
several occasions that the Wehrmacht would be in Moscow
by mid-August and that the Soviet Union would be crushed
by early October. Through the summer, the evaluations
of the OKH appeared increasingly doubtful: the strength
and fighting spirit of the Red Army had been grossly
underestimated; simultaneously, German losses were rapidly growing. The battle for Kiev, although resulting in
victory, was much harder and longer than foreseen. During
the summer, as noted above, Hitler's evaluations constantly
shifted back and forth. It is this general background which
must have led, at some stage, to his murderous decision.
Although, as we have seen from various documentary evidence, the date of mid-September remains probable, the
uncertain situation of the Russian front did not specifically
evolve in September, but constituted *the general background
for the decision*. The prolongation of the war, and especially
the growing German losses, could not but fan a mad fury
in Hitler against his enemies, particularly the internal and
universal enemy, the Jews. German blood must be avenged:
as Hitler 'prophesied', it was not the European people who
would be destroyed in a world war, but the instigators of the
war, world Jewry, who would be exterminated.

III

One may distinguish between different levels of historical
inquiry: the establishment of facts and of their immediate
links; a coherent analysis of the close historical context of
these facts; the interpretation of the close context(s) within
wider historical frameworks. The first level is necessary for
the second and the third, but neither of the interpretive levels

can be deduced from the facts alone. The second and third levels are closely linked, of necessity. The construction of the middle-range interpretations must be consonant with the main lines of the overall analysis. Moreover, the coherence of the closer reading of the historical facts must be determinant for the global interpretation, and not the other way around. Within this context, there is an obvious relation between the research presented in this book and some of the recent debates on the interpretation of Nazism and the 'Final Solution'.

In 1986 and 1987, a fierce historical-political controversy about the place of the extermination of the Jews in history and about the Nazi past in more general terms developed in Germany and beyond: it became known as 'the historians' controversy' (*Historikerstreit*).[15] The most extreme apologist position was taken by the Berlin historian Ernst Nolte, who *inter alia* argued that the Nazi extermination of the Jews was the result of Nazi fear of becoming the victims of the extermination policies which the Bolsheviks had applied from the 1917 revolution on. The Gulag was the original and Auschwitz its copy.

Burrin's detailed analysis of Hitler's view of the Jewish enemy in general and of the Jewish question during the fateful months immediately preceding and following the German attack on the Soviet Union shows that there is no apparent causal connection between Hitler's perception of Bolshevism as itself representing a danger for Germany, the German middle classes, the European bourgeoisie, and so on, and his decision to unleash the process of the extermination of the Jews. In that sense, Nolte's overall thesis does not seem to have any basis in our knowledge and interpretation of the events of the summer of 1941.

The central issue of Burrin's study is the genesis of the Final Solution in its specific context. His argument is highly coherent and excellently documented, but the indeterminacy remains. None of his arguments can be more than plausible. For instance, in following Burrin's indications of a steep increase in the killings of Jews on Soviet territory by the beginning of August 1941, one could conclude that the Goering letter, signed on the last day of July, was indeed an order to prepare for the total extermination of European Jewry, the consequences of which were immediate as far as the fate of the Soviet Jews was concerned. One could argue

as well that the Goering letter to Heydrich was the order
to prepare the total extermination, and that its first results
were noticeable, stage by stage, throughout the summer and
early autumn of 1941, until the overall plan was finalized and
agreed upon by Hitler by the end of that period, possibly in
September.

The immediate origins of the decision to implement the
total extermination of the Jews of Europe are possibly more
numerous than the causes of the prolongation of the war
on the Russian front as such, although, as Burrin himself
mentions, the various factors were intertwined and linked
to the continuing Soviet resistance. Hitler was well aware of
the increasing belligerence of the 'Judeo-capitalist' enemy,
Roosevelt's United States. After the Lend-Lease Act of the
spring of 1941 came the installation of American bases in
Iceland and the president's 'shoot-on-sight' order, as well as
the beginning of American aid to the Soviet Union. In Hitler's
view, had the Russians collapsed as anticipated, the Ameri-
cans would have been deterred from entering the war. But
the Soviet Union was fighting on and American involvement
was growing. Was not Hitler's earliest theme, of a Jewish
world conspiracy wherein capitalism and Bolshevism acted
hand in hand, finding its most concrete expression? As Burrin
clearly recognizes, the Jewish world enemy lurked in Hitler's
mind in various forms, and the themes of his first anti-Semitic
speeches reappeared as a result of the prolongation of the war
during the fateful summer and autumn of 1941.

Other elements converged with the strategic-ideological
situation. From the autumn of 1941, hundreds of thousands of Russian prisoners of war, who, until then, were
among those abandoned to starvation, were transferred to
be employed for essential economic activities in the Reich;
this decision enabled Germany to overcome the immediate
manpower difficulties which the extermination of the Jews
was bound to create.[16] Moreover, as we have seen, among
the population of the Lodz ghetto, for instance, the first
victims of extermination were those Jews who were unable
to work. Simultaneously, the SS 'solved' the problem of
overcrowding in the ghettos; Hitler's order to expel eastward
all the Jews from the major cities of the Reich could be dealt
with smoothly enough: these Jews were shot on arrival in
Riga, Kovno, Lodz, and Minsk.

In the autumn of 1941, Hitler's murderous rage did not

encounter any decisive obstacles: in addition to the executions perpetrated by the Einsatzgruppen and the setting up of the extermination site of Chelmno near Lodz, the construction of the Belsec extermination site began. The overall conditions for the 'final solution of the Jewish question in Europe' were in place.

Burrin's study belongs both to the level of factual reconstruction and to that of close interpretation. He has given us a masterful analysis – permeated with deep sensitivity – of the initially uncertain but finally implacable process which, triggered by specific circumstances, led from the ideological premisses to the murderous outcome.

Introduction

The packed trains rolling east from all over Europe, the absorption of millions of people by factories geared only to the production of corpses, the meticulous salvage of anything of use or value, the final incineration, the relentless obliteration of all traces of a human passage . . . All this – the extermination of European Jews by the Nazis – has been researched and reported by historians detailing the organization of the crime, the methods employed, the number of victims. It would be futile to try to embellish the impressive structure of their labours with yet more pages saying nothing that is not already common knowledge.[1]

But how much do we know about what preceded the slaughter? What do we know of the web of decisions and events which, one day, led to sending the first train down the track to death? Even a genocide must have some sort of birth, monstrous as that seems; it must have a genesis, though this may be rooted in events which historical investigation strains to comprehend. In the extent and forms of its carnage, in the circumstances and context of its accomplishment, the Final Solution forces the historian to acknowledge the limits of his understanding. And he concedes all the more painfully as even his knowledge lacks certainty. For several years now, a continuing debate has exposed the vulnerability of what once passed for established fact by raising again seemingly elementary questions. Did the policy of the Nazi regime inevitably lead to the Final Solution? Was the Final Solution a foregone conclusion, even for Hitler?

Many historians, and with them the enlightened public, would answer in the affirmative. Master of the Third Reich, Hitler pursued the fulfilment of a longstanding plan whose two main points were the conquest of *Lebensraum* to the east and the extermination of the Jews. The history of the Nazi regime, of course, was not one of following the marching

orders issued by an omniscient Führer. Hitler's tactical
flexibility, his talent for exploiting the opportunities as well
as the limitations of the international scene, steered his policy
into many detours – sometimes into complete reversals, such
as the signing in 1939 of the non-aggression pact with Russia.
But neither detours nor reversals caused him to deviate for
long from the direction indicated by his implacable goals.
Of course, the Nazi regime was also prey to many internal
rivalries and conflicts. But Hitler fomented these rivalries and
conflicts himself, or at least tolerated them in the game of
divide and rule. Head of a regime he controlled to the end,
he was, through his personality and theories, the prime
instigator of all the abominations the regime committed.
Animated by an incredible anti-Semitic hatred, he had had
the firm intention of killing the Jews since the 1920s; he bided
his time, and seized the moment when it came.[2]

For over ten years now, some historians have questioned
this version of events as being oversimplified. Their vision
seemed iconoclastic to many of their colleagues. Contestable
certainly, it nevertheless has made a useful contribution.[3]
According to these historians, whose relatively less-known
viewpoint merits greater exposure, the Third Reich, when
one considers its day-to-day operation, seems to have functioned as an 'authoritarian anarchy'.[4] Behind the sleek,
monolithic facade presented by its propaganda machine,
Nazi power was frustrated and thwarted by a network of
rival forces: traditional power centres like the administration
and the army, and new factions, represented by the party
and its subsidiaries, which fed off every organization that
had not already been eliminated. Thus the SS absorbed the
police while chipping away at the army's monopoly. In this
dog-eat-dog atmosphere, the regime's policy was structurally
doomed to a shifting course and to improvisation. How many
decisions must have been made without the slightest thought
to their long-term effects! And how many were reached
through compromise between rival factions, so that the
initial intent, if there had been one, was lost in the process.

Incontestably, the regime centred on one man. Hitler was
the sun of the system, he dispensed the power and the
favours, he smiled or frowned on questions of ideology.
There was no doubt that he adhered fanatically to the
racist formulas he proclaimed. But these formulas made
up a confused ideological mix, from which he could not

easily derive clear objectives; the intensity of the hatred did not compensate for the relative inconsistency of the concepts. The policy of the Third Reich, in any case, seems too incoherent to have been guided by a master plan. Furthermore, even if Hitler had had one, his executive style would have hampered its implementation. It was the Führer's habit to parcel out responsibilities among his lieutenants without unduly bothering to define them, or simply to rubber-stamp proposals or endorse initiatives from his underlings. Concerned above all with preserving his prestige, he reacted to the incessant conflicts that were the price of his behaviour by letting time heal them rather than by taking sides. His role, in sum, was essentially indirect: through his ideological tirades he channelled and inflamed the competition between the different factions of his regime, a competition which resulted in a continuous radicalization.

The conduct of the policy towards the Jews offers a perfect example. When one examines it closely, it seems anything but linear, and hardly suggests the existence of an extermination plan. Up until the war began and even afterwards, as late as 1941, the departure of Jews from the Reich was the goal pursued by Nazi leaders. Yet it was these same Jews they had tried so hard to disperse which, after 1941, they would have to retrieve from all over Europe in order to kill. If Hitler had been harbouring an extermination plan, should he not have prevented these departures and kept his victims on hand for the day of reckoning?

In reality, he did not have a plan, but only an obsession: to cleanse the Reich of the Jews within its borders, whose number multiplied with each conquest. But all the paths he took stopped short of his goal. The emigration policy was frustrated by the outbreak of war. The plan to create a Jewish reservation on Madagascar was scuttled by the ongoing war with England. And finally, the conquest of Russia, which was to have opened up new territories for the resettlement of Jews, soon ran up against the resistance of the Soviet army, after some early victories which occasioned premature deportations. Caught in this new impasse, local authorities, fired by the Führer's hate-filled pronouncements, avoided overcrowding the ghettos in the East by executing all those unable to work. This makeshift solution eventually won the approval of the supreme authority. Since there was nowhere for them to be sent, the Jews would vanish by the only remaining route: death. The Final Solution was born, then, of the confluence of the Führer's anti-Semitic obsession, the anarchic operation of his regime, and the emergence of an uncontrollable situation.[5]

The battlelines could not be more clearly drawn: two interpretations, each claiming to explain how the Final Solution came about. According to the first, currently called intentionalist, the extermination of the Jews was the fulfilment of a plan, the plan of a man with absolute power. According to the second, termed functionalist, it was the result of a persecution process thrown out of control by the dynamic of a regime not only fundamentally irrational but also incapable of anything but increasingly radical improvisation.

The dispute extends into the realm of dates. For the intentionalists, the turning-point was some time between the autumn of 1940 and late spring of 1941; it was in this time-frame, during preparations for the Russian campaign, that Hitler gave the order that would bring to fruition the plan he had harboured for years. For the functionalists, on the other hand, the turning-point was in the autumn of 1941, with the outbreak of executions on a local level, sanctioned after the fact by Hitler and escalated into an operation on a European scale. Small as the discrepancy may seem, it is nevertheless significant in that it concerns an event of such magnitude. It symbolizes the uncertainty of our knowledge about the manner in which millions of people were condemned to death, fifty years ago.

This state of affairs can be explained primarily by the great gaps in documentation. No document survives bearing an extermination order signed by Hitler, nor any document attesting to the existence of such a written order. In all likelihood, the orders were verbal ones; it is known that the enterprise was shrouded in conditions of secrecy. In any case, nothing palpable has surfaced to shed light on how the decision evolved or on its chronology. The deepest mystery surrounds the content of the conversations between Hitler and his chief of police, Himmler, during the course of that fatal year, 1941. The historian always works from evidence; the evidence here is not only sparse but also difficult to interpret: even the expression 'Final Solution' changed meaning over the years. A no less formidable obstacle is presented by the assessment of the motives and behaviour of Hitler, an aberrant personality in many respects, certainly in his monstrous criminality. It is easier for us to explore the intimate thoughts of a Churchill or a Roosevelt, but how can we be sure we have grasped those of a Hitler?

The conflict of interpretations exists, then; but there is no reason to settle for it. The debate pitting these arguments against each other has had the advantage of pointing up their respective merits and limitations, and of locating and clarifying the ongoing problems.[6] As the functionalists have emphasized, by too closely linking the genocide to Hitler's personality and intentions we lose sight of the effect of context, of the role of circumstance, and of the significance of a whole series of factors not in the power of one man to create or even to control. The Final Solution is inexplicable unless we take into account the joint contribution of all factions of the regime, and notably of the conservative elite, whose support was crucial to the establishment of the Nazi dictatorship and the commission of its heinous crimes.

More fundamentally, the intentionalist thesis tends to exaggerate the coherence of Hitler's ideology, and to present in an absolute light his ability to issue unequivocal directives for action. Furthermore, it neglects or minimizes the fact that Nazi policy changed course when it replaced emigration/expulsion with extermination. To draw a straight line from the 1920s to Auschwitz, one must assume a tenacious Machiavellism in Hitler: that is the only way to reconcile the allegation of an early extermination plan with the divergent policy conducted by his regime.

But if the functionalists have stressed the complexity and the sinuosity of the course of history, they have also swung the pendulum to the opposite extreme. For, ultimately, the question here is not whether Hitler alone is responsible for the Holocaust; it is whether, in 1941, under the existing conditions, the genocide could have occurred without his impetus, and whether that impetus derived from an ideology consistent enough to provide direction and purpose. To demonstrate that Hitler was the prisoner of a regime of which he was the formal head, the functionalist argument must also rest on an assumption: that of the irrelevance of Hitler's murderous declarations to the policy of extermination conducted by the Third Reich.

Of course Hitler wavered at times; he often temporized,

and readily delegated the conduct of various matters to subordinates. And, of course, many of the regime's decisions were made in a confused way, without the Führer's visible participation. But these facts are only valid within certain limits. Hitler personally monitored and supervised foreign policy and military strategy every step of the way. Despite the gaps in documentation, it is demonstrable that his participation became more active, and his control more absolute, the closer the issue approached the heart of his convictions, one of which, of course, was the famous Jewish question. The role of 'great men' is rightly regarded with suspicion by a history concerned with the broader picture. Nevertheless, this is a case in which one man played a pivotal part.[7]

The essential challenge emerging from the debate is to articulate Hitler's role and the change of course that occurred in his regime's policy. We can detect an increasing convergence among historians who have recently addressed the issue, and even agreement on two points. First, given the regime's operational procedures, the launching of the genocide could only have been effected through a central control, under Hitler's direction. Secondly, the decision probably was not reached overnight, but matured over a period of transition before being finalized some time between the summer and the autumn, rather than the spring, of 1941. Beyond that, serious fundamental disagreements still remain, as we can see by examining the positions of three historians who have recently contributed to the study of the subject.

The German historian Eberhard Jäckel, who in a now classic work stressed the coherence of Hitler's ideology, concedes today that it was not without contradictions, and that this measure of incoherence might have made it difficult to set priorities. He still thinks that Hitler had the intention of exterminating the Jews, although he no longer explicitly states it. That inner will, in any case, was carried out with an uncertain step, due to the extraordinary nature of the enterprise. Hitler had to induce his lieutenants to do something they had never done before, or even imagined doing. He had to proceed with caution, feeling out the territory, 'initiating' the faithful one by one. He was Machievellian but also fallible, since he would twice misread the situation: in the autumn of 1939 he would underestimate, and in the summer of 1941 overestimate, the difficulties standing in the way of embarking on genocide. Hence the circuitous and largely improvised path to the Final Solution. In this interpretation, which aims at reconciling improvisation and premeditation, Hitler's intention remains central; circumstances recede into the background, insignificant except in relation to the association which existed, in the Führer's mind, between genocide and the conduct of the war.[8]

On the other side, the American historian Christopher Browning, who describes himself as a moderate functionalist, believes that the extermination of the Jews was not one of Hitler's goals in the 1920s and 1930s. If he finally gave the order, it was due to the failure of other solutions he had tried to implement and to his ensuing frustration. The experiments carried out in 1940–41 would have led to a radicalization of the genocidal impulse clearly present in his ideology, but not yet crystallized into a programme. At the prospect of inheriting millions more Jews after the triumph of a Russian conquest, a Hitler driven by the obsession to purify the Third Reich, and pushed to his limits by his earlier failures, would have opted for extermination.[9]

Arno Mayer, finally, has recently proposed an explanation that belongs, as does Browning's, to the functionalist school. In his opinion, anti-Semitism was just one component of Hitler's ideology, along with anti-Bolshevism and expansionism to the East. It is thus doubtful that Hitler could have evolved a programme of extermination. When he plunged into genocide, it was more likely in response to the failure of the Russian campaign which was also the failure of a crusade vested, for the first time, with all the elements of his ideology. Differing from Browning, who links the decision for extermination to a climate of triumph and euphoria, Mayer sees in the failure of the Russian campaign the combination of circumstances that gave birth to the Holocaust.[10]

Thus a quite distinct polarity remains between the two basic interpretations: on the one hand, extermination by intention, on the other, radicalization through circumstances. Retracing the path to the Final Solution, I would support another explanation in which the two existing approaches are combined. Like the intentionalists, I believe that Hitler harboured the intention of exterminating the Jews; this intention, however, was not absolute, but conditional: it would be carried out only in the event of a well-defined situation, such as the failure of his planned conquests, leaving the way clear to pursue meanwhile another policy. Like the functionalists, on the other hand, I maintain that a combination of circumstances was essential to the fulfilment of this intention, for its translation into action: here the perception of the failure of the Russian campaign and of its strategic consequences played a decisive part.

In the following pages, I restrict the perspective to what seems necessary to my purpose. The focus is on high-ranking Nazi officials, primarily on Hitler himself, on his theories and intentions, and also on his evaluation of the strategic situation. Many aspects of the picture have been left in shadow, or even in darkness: the historical roots of anti-Semitism, the attitudes of the German elite, and the short-sighted policy of the Western powers. More crucially, the victims themselves will virtually be absent, except as the objects of an unprecedented persecution. The reader will bear in mind that these objects were human beings, exposed to blows and humiliations, to the progressive deprivation of their property, and sometimes of their dignity, until their departure, one day, for the death factories.

1

Hitler's Anti-Semitism

Hitler occupied a key position in the Third Reich and was a fanatical anti-Semite. On these two points all historians agree, regardless of whatever disagreements they may have about the actual part he played. A familiarity with his ideology, in particular with his anti-Semitism, is therefore essential. What position did the Jews occupy in it, and to what fate did it doom them? That Hitler was capable of exterminating them he amply demonstrated. But we can only illuminate the origins and motives of his attitude by starting with the vision of the world that guided him.

The essential factor, which must be stressed at the outset, is the astonishing consistency and continuity of that world vision, once it was fully formed. As far back as the early 1920s, when Hitler was just a Bavarian agitator, its familiar leitmotifs were already blaring forth: racism and anti-Semitism, the ideal of the centralized national community, the leader principle, the unconditional condemnation of democracy, of the German revolution, and of the Treaty of Versailles. In 1923 another theme was added, that of the conquest of Lebensraum to the East, rounded out a little later by a global concept of foreign policy.

From then on, everything that has survived of Hitler's public and private statements, up to his testament of April 1945, attests to the permanence of a vision tirelessly reiterated and proclaimed. Certain themes, it is true, were modulated over the years. The conquest of Lebensraum and the concept of anti-Semitism, very much present in the 1920s, faded into the background at the end of the decade, especially from 1930 to 1932, when Hitler was striving to rally as much public support as possible. But, significantly, they did not disappear.[1] On the other hand, his theories on the fate of future conquered peoples – expulsion or sterilization of entire populations, the reduction of millions of persons to illiterate slavery – would be reserved for his entourage and for the party's high command.[2]

At the basis of the Hitlerian world vision was the 'eternal principle of natural selection', a theory in which the stronger race was supposed to assert and impose its will on the weaker. For Hitler, humankind was composed of races as separate from one another as species in the animal kingdom. Within these races was a hierarchy determined by historical greatness, an ever-precarious hierarchy: only pure-bloodedness assured a race's continued standing. Through ignorance of these 'eternal lessons of nature', the German people had fallen into decadence, a decadence that began with the creation of the Bismarckian empire and whose symptoms, in addition to the loss of national values to debilitating ideologies such as liberalism, democracy, and Marxism, were the spread of venereal and hereditary diseases and, finally, 'crossbreeding' with inferior races.

To snatch the German race from the jaws of decadence, it was necessary to purify it and to have it propagate. From the early 1920s Hitler had talked of outlawing marriages between Germans and foreigners, particularly blacks and Jews. But the fight against crossbreeding would require more radical forms of cleansing. As he told an American magazine reporter in 1923, Germany needed drastic remedies, perhaps even 'amputations'. Syphilitics, alcoholics, and criminals must be isolated and sterilized. A single motto should inspire the action: 'The preservation of the nation is more important than the preservation of these unfortunates'.[3]

Hitler reiterated these goals in *Mein Kampf*, writing of 'making the most weighty and most trenchant decisions'. It would come, 'if necessary, to the strict isolation of incurables, a barbaric measure for those unfortunate enough to be afflicted, but a blessing for their contemporaries and for posterity'. The racist state of the future would forbid procreation to individuals known to be sick or suffering from hereditary defects, and would 'physically remove their reproductive capacity'.[4] He would, on the other hand, encourage marriage and a high birth-rate by fighting abortion and restoring the large family to a place of honour. He would do everything, finally, to realize 'that supreme good: a race created according to the rules of eugenics'.[5]

This rebuilding of the race was not an end in itself but a means to an end: the power and glory of the German people. After restoring political unity to the nation, and undertaking the work of racial purification, it would then be possible to embark on the conquest of the space necessary for the nation's welfare. The German people, according to Hitler, had a right to expansion because of the discrepancy between the numerical size of its population and the extent of its land – a specious argument since the future regime would seek to increase that population by every available means. Thus, quite openly, if not world domination, certainly the domination of Europe was the target. As Hitler wrote on the last page of his book: 'a state which, in a time of racial contamination, jealously watches over the best elements of its own race, must one day become master of the earth'.[6]

The Jews could not be absent from this racist theory. In Hitler's eyes, they were a parasite race which exploited the labour of the people among whom they settled; a race destructive by nature, incapable of establishing its own state; a race whose every activity was geared to the acquisition of world domination. For, as *The Protocols of the Elders of Zion*, that fake tsarist tract in which Hitler blindly believed, was supposed to prove, the Jews were bound together by a plot to dominate the world, and would stoop to anything to reach their goal. The ideas of the Enlightenment, democracy, pacifism, anything served that weakened the national will of the people off whom they lived. But their most effective tools were financial capital and Marxist agitation. By means of the first, they internationalized economies and brought them under their control. By means of the second, they divided people against each other and doomed them to civil wars that destroyed their powers of resistance. In one way or another, they were the enemies of any real national independence.

Hitler's anti-Semitism was a fantastic concept that completely ignored the diversity of the Jewish diaspora and the conflicting movements that accompanied it; and yet a coherent fantasy, inspired as it was by an obsessive search for the ultimate culprit, some evil principle that would explain the workings of the universe and shed light on the calamities of the times. But hardly an original fantasy, and hardly personal. Hitler was the direct heir of theories that had been circulating through Europe for several decades. But while he had patched his racist doctrine together with borrowed concepts, he had also integrated it into a world vision that singularly energized it and remodeled certain of its aspects. Seen in the framework of his racism, the 'Jewish problem' was a problem among others, a problem whose solution would contribute to restoring and strengthening the nation. In reality, however, Jews were not in the same category as mental defectives: they were at the centre of Hitler's vision of the world. To understand the specificity of his anti-Semitism, one must consider the existential source that inspired it and gave it its texture: the experience of the First World War and of Germany's defeat.

It was this defeat that gave Hitler's undertaking its fundamental impetus. In *Mein Kampf* he recorded the enthusiasm with which he greeted the outbreak of war in August 1914. In total contrast was the extreme rage that seized him at the time of the surrender, a surrender which seemed to him the product of betrayal from the rear. A clearly traumatic experience: throughout his career he would return to the events of November 1918 as a central reference point, always evoking them with an emotionally charged intensity. He dated his entry into politics back to the 'frightful days' of the German revolution. They were what launched him on 'the search for the causes of the German collapse,' and made him see the necessity of a political movement whose goal would be 'to triumph over the defeat'.[7] They served as a frame of reference for future action, and created enduring mental attitudes.

It is impossible to exaggerate the extent to which Hitler was marked by the war and the defeat. From them came his conviction that the workers must be won back to the nation, and that the ruling classes were bankrupt. From them he also derived the strategic principles that would later guide him. In his opinion the German Empire's cardinal mistake was to have united the other European powers against it when its only ally was an Austro-Hungary on the verge of collapse. Wisdom would have dictated winning over England by abandoning a naval strategy that threatened her, and by giving priority, at least temporarily, to continental rather than to colonial expansion. In the future, everything must be done to avert the formation of such a coalition. The 'New Germany' would need allies, which would be Italy and Great Britain.

To win the first, as early as the 1920s Hitler declared himself ready to give up the Southern Tyrol; he reaffirmed on many occasions his hope of forming an alliance with the second. Evidently, he failed to appreciate the seriousness of British opposition to any continental hegemony. Once in power, he persisted in seeking to win London over to his way of thinking, at first by negotiation, later by force.

But the acquisition of allies was only a means: it was supposed to provide the freedom of action necessary for advancing, by localized wars, towards the larger objective. The first victim would be France, Germany's eternal enemy. Once its back was secure, the Reich would embark on the conquest of the vast territories to the East: there it would find the means of feeding its population and establishing its position as a world power. Localized blitzkriegs were the ideal strategy, one that took into account the limitations of the German economy and avoided overburdening the population: here again the lesson of 1918 had been learned. Conversely, everything must be done to prevent a war on two fronts which, Hitler was deeply persuaded, would once again prove fatal to Germany.

Furthermore, from his vision of the Great War and the defeat Hitler drew lifelong convictions. The first followed from his absolute belief that the war was lost because of the weakness of the imperial government, a victim of unneccessary if not criminal humanitarian concerns. He would have settled his score with Marxism before the outbreak of hostilities by turning the patriotic fervour of the workers to his advantage. He would have severely punished saboteurs of the war effort and inflicted the harshest penalties on the 'sinister gangs' of 'criminals', 'pimps', and 'deserters' who, according to him, later controlled the events of November 1918. Finally, he would have ruthlessly suppressed the revolution itself, even if it meant executing thousands of people.[8]

From which he concluded:

before conquering the enemies without, one must have exterminated the enemy within; or else, woe to the people whose efforts are not crowned with victory from the first day. It is enough that the shadow of defeat pass over a people which has harboured enemy elements in its breast; its powers of resistance will be broken, and the enemy without will carry the day.[9]

He drew another conclusion from the experience of 1918. He was convinced that the armistice had been a major mistake, that the war could have been won if a man determined to fight to the end had been at the head of the country, a man capable of galvanizing and stiffening the nation's morale. Even if it was hopeless, the fight should have been carried on. Victory or death was a motto he cherished. After 1939, as we shall see, he repeated *ad nauseam* that a surrender would not happen again.

The defeat also had a traumatizing effect on Hitler's anti-Semitism, endowing it with extraordinary virulence and elevating it into a central obsession. Doubtless it was in Vienna before the war that he became, as he wrote, 'a fanatical anti-Semite'.[10] But we can suppose that his was a still largely intellectual anti-Semitism, albeit one based on a considerable foundation of resentments. Significantly, it is in the passage in his book where he relates his reaction to the events of November 1918 that he uses the word 'hate': it was then that 'hate was born in me, hate for the perpetrators of these events'. This passage was followed a few lines later by this conclusion: 'With the Jew, there can be no negotiation, but only the decision: all or nothing! As for me, I have decided to go into politics.'[11] Very probably, it was at that moment that Hitler's anti-Semitism became an existential obsession, charged with the hate that would henceforth characterize it. It was at that moment also that it assumed a central position in his world vision, providing him with an explanation for the defeat.

Hitler viewed the defeat as the culmination of a war waged pitilessly by the Jews, an internal as well as an external war. Jews living abroad had fomented hatred of Germany and driven the whole world into the conflict. Meanwhile, inside Germany, their brothers had seized control of the economy and incited the workers to revolution; when the time came, they were able to stab Germany in the back. They were therefore responsible for the defeat and the 'slavery' imposed by the Treaty of Versailles. The struggle against them would end only in total victory for one side or the other.

In a logical fashion, the Jews occupied a major position in Hitler's concept of foreign policy. The previously designated enemies of the 'New Germany' were the USSR and France. In Russia, 'the Jew' had reigned supreme since he seized power under the cloak of communism and exterminated the old ruling classes of German origin. Since he was incapable of constructive work, the regime he dominated was 'ripe for collapse'[12] – an underestimation Hitler would entertain until 1941. In France, a mutual understanding reigned between the national elite and the Jews, of one mind in their implacable hostility towards Germany and in their determination to reduce her to slavery. On the other hand, the situation in the countries Hitler wanted as allies was better, though by no means assured. In Italy, Mussolini was thought to be firmly enough in the saddle to be able to protect the true interests of his country from the pressures of Jewry. The situation was less favourable in England where, as in the United States, Jewish influence was considered strong. From the beginning, Hitler believed that the outcome of his future efforts to win Britain as an ally would depend on the battle in London between the national and Jewish forces; he had an explanation ready for every outcome.

A global struggle was thus engaged between the force of national renewal, with Hitler at its head, and an 'international Jewry' bent on the destruction of Germany. Whence the presence in Hitler's anti-Semitism of a quasi-internationalist vein that expressed itself upon occasion through the slogan: 'Anti-Semites of the world, unite!'[13] Whence also the existence of a messianic vein: Hitler presented himself as the man who had been given the task of ridding the earth of the Jewish peril.[14] Against this global adversary he would put up an almost religious fight, a 'titanic struggle' that would culminate in sending back 'to hell he who mounts an assault on heaven'.[15]

The essential idea, here as in all Hitler's arguments, ran thus: the Jew was rising up against the world order; he was the rebel and the aggressor; it was he who sought to destroy Germany and even to exterminate her population. Against this monstrous menace Hitler merely reacted: as he loved to point out, his struggle was purely defensive, imposed on him by the threat of extinction the Jews held over the German people.[16] This easily recognizable characteristic is central to the nationalism of the extreme right: the perception of oneself and one's conduct as responses to a diabolical plot or menace. It is a perception we would be wrong to underestimate: in Hitler's eyes, measures taken against the Jews would always be measures of self-defence or prevention, justified by a mortal danger. It is also a concept that was an integral part of his mind-set. As the philologist Klemperer noted, Hitler's statements constantly reveal the interaction of a Caesarean megalomania with a persecution complex.[17]

Anti-Semitism occupied thus an exceptional place in Hitler's racism. Doctrinally, the Jewish problem represented one aspect of the racial purification programme he intended to carry out in Germany as soon as he had seized power; it was therefore susceptible to a cold, rational solution. On the other hand, it lay at the heart of his plan for conquest and domination. In the interpretation he gave of the trauma of the defeat, the Jew had been elevated to the rank of ultimate adversary; he had become fundamentally linked to the fate of Hitler's plan, to its success or failure. Therefore, the Jewish problem was destined to dog Hitler's footsteps until the end of his crusade, and the Jews to suffer its dire consequences.

But what fate did Hitler hold in store for the Jews? Had he decided in principle on their extermination? Among his avowed goals, no clue is to be found. In 1919 he proclaimed the necessity for an anti-Semitism of reason, based on the recognition of the Jewish problem as a racial problem, in preference to an anti-Semitism of sentiment which could only lead to pogroms. He proposed combating the Jews with legal and systematic measures which would classify them under legislation applicable to foreigners, the ultimate goal being their deportation from the country.[18] The February 1920 programme of the Nazi party provided for legislation along the same lines, without calling for the expulsion of all Jews. Citizenship would be reserved for Germans by race; Jews would be excluded from public service and from the press, but only those who had emigrated to Germany after 2 August 1914 would be expelled. Point 7, however, specified that it was the duty of the state to proceed 'in case of need' with the expulsion of all foreigners.

In the propaganda campaign waged by Hitler during the following years we find these same demands, with the same variations. Sometimes it was only a question of deporting Jews who had recently come to Europe from the East (the *Ostjuden*) and of banning all further immigration.[19] More frequently, the deportation of all Jews was demanded, habitually under the slogan 'Jews Out'. In December 1928 Hitler once more declared that they would only be tolerated in Germany 'as foreigners'.[20] This was the extent of his liberality: in the best of cases, Jews would have a precarious status, but for how long? If it is difficult to gain a clear and complete picture of his intentions, one can, however, justify saying that he had decided, once in power, to enforce a certain number of measures. Jews would be excluded from public service and from all positions which could influence national life; in due course they would have to disappear from German territory, probably after having been divested of their worldly goods.[21]

Hitler clearly found it difficult to articulate a programme. Although he held forth in *Mein Kampf* about the goals of his foreign policy, detailing its methods and stages, he never said a word about the steps he would take, once in power, concerning the Jews, designated as a principal adversary throughout the work. An explanation can be found in the fact that the Jews occupied too central and too intensely emotional a place in his vision to become the subjects of a programme. A second explanation relates to the nature of the Jewish problem – that it was not just a German problem. As he declared to Rauschning in the early 1930s: 'Even when we have chased the Jew from Germany, he will still remain our global enemy.'[22]

Thus a tension, if not a contradiction, could arise between the policy of the removal of the Jews, which would solve the problem in Germany, and the policy that called for fighting a global enemy. If the battle waged against the Jews in Germany triggered the hostility of their brothers throughout the world (and of this Hitler was already convinced), it was unthinkable for him not to respond to the challenge: what better response than to use the German Jews as hostages? It was at the end of 1922 that he expressed this idea for the first time. After he assumed power, the Jews would be held as hostages until non-aggression pacts were concluded with foreign countries: in other words, until the international security of the new regime was assured.[23] His behaviour as well as his declarations would show that this concept was deeply rooted in his mind.

The removal of the Jews would, therefore, be weighed against the necessity of keeping them as hostages, at least for a while. In the end, however, it was the first objective that was supposed to be implemented. But Hitler could not settle for it pure and simple; a global solution would have to be found that would override its disadvantages and defuse

the Jewish peril once and for all. The Zionist solution did
not have his approval, even though he sometimes said that
the Jews belonged in Palestine rather than in Germany. He
doubted that the Jews seriously intended to assemble in
one state, their objective being, rather, to create a centre
that would guarantee them state protection everywhere in
the world. What was the answer, then? According to the
memoirs of one of his old intimates, Hitler declared in 1931
that the global power of Jewry could only be broken by the
deportation of all Jews to a Jewish state. But this would
require the co-operation of all the countries in the world,
which was not going to happen tomorrow.[24] Here we see
the emergence of the concept of a Jewish reservation, the
concentration of Jews in a territory that would be placed
under surveillance. Reduced to being at the planet's mercy,
they would no longer endanger it.

Extermination is absent from all this. It is conceivable, however, that such an objective could not be spoken. According
to evidence released after the war, Hitler declared in 1922, in
the course of a private conversation, that once in power he
would hang all the Jews in Germany in the public squares
and let them rot.[25] No other source confirms these remarks
which, in the context in which they were made, seem to have
more in common with a death wish than with a programme.
We lack elements of direct proof, but the exploration of
indirect approaches remains open to us. Hitler's vision of
the world, like his vocabulary, had implications that must
be taken into consideration.

Hitler, as we have seen, viewed his war against the Jews
as a battle for the salvation of the world, a fight to the
death that could only end with the extinction of one of the
two adversaries. He also stressed on many occasions that
this battle would be violent. Evoking the Jewish design of
world domination, he wrote that no nation could 'remove
this hand from its throat save by the sword', which would
not happen 'without bloodshed'.[26] When he talked about the
Jews, he usually hurled imprecations and turned readily to
the language of destruction; the enemy must be struck down
ruthlessly and annihilated.[27] He constantly used a vocabulary
that dehumanized Jews and implied that they should be
physically eliminated: microbes, parasites, leeches, spiders
– so much harmful or repulsive vermin where extermination
brings relief.

In another sense, there was nothing personal about this language; it belonged to an anti-Semitic tradition which, in fact, was not properly German: in the France of the Dreyfus affair, the same comparison with vermin accompanied quite specific calls for bloodshed.[28] And Hitler often used the term 'Jews' in a vague manner, applying it to all his enemies, particularly to Marxists, so that it is not always easy to determine exactly to whom his threats referred: to the Jewish community specifically or to an amalgam of his political adversaries?

It remains true, however, that the figure of the Jewish adversary aroused considerable hatred in him, and that a massacre was permanently etched on his mind's horizon. It nevertheless seems excessive to me to infer from this that his unconditional objective was to exterminate the Jews, unless we simply equate a murderous potential and a murderous intent.[29] To do this, however, would be to block the possibility of understanding a crucial aspect of the problem. For that murderous potential, so present and yet in a way so imprecise as to its target and scope, does seem to border on intent in one very specific context.

We have already stressed the intense hate Hitler breathed into his statements whenever he referred to 1918. It is precisely in these passages evoking the November revolution that he expressed most concretely, and with the greatest emotional force, his desire for a bloody settling of accounts with the Jews. Thus, after having mentioned the enthusiasm of the German workers in the summer of 1914, and their detachment from the Marxist leaders, he wrote:

> That would have been the moment to take action against the whole two-faced conspiracy of Jewish corrupters of the people. That is when, unhesitatingly, we should have moved against them, without the slightest regard for whatever cries and lamentations they might have raised. . . . While the best of us were dying at the front, at least we should have disposed of the vermin in the rear.[30]

And further on, still on the subject of the evil influence of the Marxist leaders who (according to him) were all Jews:

> If just once, at the beginning or during the course of the war, we had exposed twelve or fifteen thousand of those Hebrew corruptors of the people to the poison gas that hundreds of thousands of our best German workers of every

extraction and every profession had to endure at the front, the sacrifice of millions of men would not have been in vain. On the contrary, if we had rid ourselves of those twelve or so thousand fiends, we perhaps might have saved the lives of a million good, brave Germans full of promise.[31]

These passages are reproduced regularly as evidence of Hitler's will to exterminate, which seems to me to ask a great deal of the text and, above all, to ignore its central meaning. As we have said, Hitler had derived from his experience the conviction that in future the nation must be purified before going to war. But in the passages we have just quoted, he sees things from a different perspective, in that he returns to a past war to evoke what, after all, could have been done. Writing after the defeat, he retrospectively attributes a twofold value to the expedient step he wishes had been taken. A propitiatory value, for a step of this kind, expressing a desire to fight to the death, might 'perhaps' have brought victory, thus saving the lives of many German soldiers. A vengeance value, and this is the most striking: the deaths of thousands of Jews, even if they had not changed the outcome of the war, would have been fully justified, in that they would have avenged the Germans fallen at the front.

By making such an association, between a long war, which spilled German blood and threatened to end in defeat, and the murder of a certain number of Jews, was Hitler in his rage simply reinterpreting the past, or was he also finding solutions for the future? To the degree that it is true that he approached the future with fixed conclusions drawn from the war and the defeat, we must also see in his statements a determination to apply them if the same situation should arise. This is confirmed in the following assertion, made in 1931, according to a source whose authenticity, admittedly, is open to question:

We have learned a great deal from the last war and in the future we shall reap the benefits. (*Here Hitler suddenly flew into a rage and continued with vehemence:*) In a case where our legitimate purpose is not understood and where the armed conflict is once again caused by world Jewry trying to turn back the pages of history . . . then they will be crushed.[32]

We could maintain, then – and this hypothesis will be subjected to verification in the following chapters – that in Hitler's attitude toward the Jews a homicidal potential

escalated into a murderous intent, and even into an extermination plan, although we cannot be sure of this, only in
one case: the recurrence of a long war, a world war. Such
a situation would signal the failure of his whole strategy,
to be achieved by means of blitzkriegs. It would portend,
furthermore, another triumph for the Jews, who had already
been the victors in the Great War. In such an event, he vowed
to take radical action against those he believed to be his
ultimate adversaries: that action would demonstrate his will
to fight to victory or to the death, would make the Jews pay
for spilled German blood, and would avenge by anticipation
the defeat that another war against a world coalition would
probably cost Germany.

Here again we find the tension, if not the outright contradiction, already mentioned. Whether from Germany or from
the future Great Reich, the departure of the Jews was
imperative: they posed a grave danger to racial purity and to
national cohesion. They therefore had to be removed quickly,
if possible before the outbreak of another conflict, if possible
by finding an international solution like a reservation, which
would render them harmless. On the other hand, their
presence in the German sphere would guarantee Hitler a
means of pressuring 'international Jewry' as he faced the
challenges of his first days in power, and would also assure
that he had an object of vengeance at hand in the event
that his global strategy failed. As far as we can tell, neither
of these two considerations had priority: they coexisted in
his mind, creating a true ambivalence that sprang from
his obsessive will to fight against an allegedly worldwide
enemy.

This ambivalence probably contributed to the difficulty he
had in formulating a programme. He had no such trouble
with the conquest of Lebensraum, an objective more easily
kept at a mental remove. But regarding the Jews, he was
reduced to a mass of heterogeneous attitudes and resolutions which could collide when it came to formulating
a programme. Lebensraum and the Jewish problem were
inseparable, although they bore a changing relationship to
one another. Since the conquest of Lebensraum was the
primary goal, the fight against the Jewish peril must not
be pursued to the point of jeopardizing it: once victory
was assured, the Jews would be reduced to helplessness
in any case. But if the conquest of Lebensraum failed, the

radical fight against the Jews could become the primary goal, substituting for the first in order to avenge its failure.

The most striking thing is that Hitler seems, from the beginning, to have envisioned his failure and settled on a reaction to it. Even before assuming power, he brooded over the conclusions drawn from his wartime experience: there would not be another revolution; there would not be another surrender; finally, the Jews would pay dearly for any further opposition to the Reich's march to domination. In view of his personality and the fantastic logic of his anti-Semitism, it seems improbable to me that Hitler had in mind an extermination plan that would be put into effect in every instance, including an eventual victory. The success of his undertaking would prove that the Jews were not, after all, as powerful as he had imagined: their placement under surveillance in a reservation would suffice; they would be the living proof of his triumph. On the other hand, their satanic nature would be confirmed in the event of lack of success; he would then react in even more extreme fashion since he would have the sense of an even greater menace, an even more disastrous end to his ambition.

Hitler was not alone in this way of thinking. The idea of treating Jews as hostages, and of extracting reprisals from them that would grow harsher as the situation worsened, seems to have been widespread among Germans of the extreme right after the war, although a systematic study of this subject remains to be done. For men convinced of the existence of a world Jewry, it went without saying that in the future the Jewish population would have to suffer the consequences for any assault on the fatherland, or the men who claimed to personify it. Thus Goebbels threatened on 19 September 1930 to launch a pogrom if an attempt was made on the life of a Nazi leader. On 21 March 1933, shortly after Hitler assumed power, a Leipzig newspaper carried this warning: 'If a bullet strikes our beloved leader, all the Jews in Germany will immediately be put up against the wall and the result will be a greater bloodbath than anything the world has ever seen!'[33] Other Nazis spoke, during the same period, of exterminating the German Jews if the French crossed the frontier, or announced, in the most general terms, that if a foreign army dared to tread upon German soil, it would have to march across the corpses of Jews.[34]

Hitler was no doubt exceptional in the pathological intensity of his anti-Semitism. Nevertheless, in his obsessions and
attitudes, he echoed the thinking of a number of men who,
like him, had shifted the tactics of war into the field of political
action, and had fashioned from the trauma of defeat a fantasy
of apocalyptic violence in which the Jews were the targets
of choice. We can speculate that, at the dawn of the Third
Reich, these men faced the future armed with at least one
certainty: another defeat would not occur except at horrible
cost to the Jews.

2

The Emigration Policy, 1933–1939

In 1933, Hitler was called on by President Hindenburg to form a government of 'national concentration'. Few contemporaries would have hazarded a guess as to the duration of the new cabinet. Hitler was flanked by a majority of representatives from the conservative right, who counted on keeping him on a tight rein. They paid dearly for this illusion, thanks to the formidable tools given him by his party, and thanks also to their own spinelessness. In a few months Hitler had silenced any support for them that might have been used against him. After the dissolution of all political and syndicalist organizations, the Nazi party emerged as the sole force in power. It undertook to police the people, and to indoctrinate them with the new national and racial gospel.

Hitler's power was just in its infancy. His first decisions, such as Germany's withdrawal from the Conference on Disarmament and from the League of Nations, were voted on by plebiscite. Soon the rising economy, boosted by massive rearmament, brought the return of full employment and assured his popularity. His bloody purge of the recalcitrant leadership of the storm-troopers only increased it. Hindenburg's death, in August 1934, permitted him to add the title of President of the Reich to his office, and thereby to become commander-in-chief of the armed forces. By that time, several conservative figures had left the government, after realizing the insane delusion of their domestication plan. In early 1938, the last two conservative ministers of any importance departed: the Minister of War, Blomberg, whose duties were taken over by Hitler himself, and the Minister of Foreign Affairs, Neurath, who was replaced by von Ribbentrop. The cabinet had stopped meeting as of November 1937; virtually nothing stood in Hitler's way.

Since his nomination, he had pressed toward the realization of his fundamental objective: the recovery of Germany
and the achievement of European hegemony. He had also
embarked, with the same zeal, on translating his anti-
Semitism into acts. In the six years before the outbreak of
war, a flood of measures was passed which resulted in the
growing persecution of Jews living in Germany. But they
were adopted in such great disorder that some historians
have been led to doubt that Hitler had a political direction,
or that he did much more than endorse the anarchic spiral
of persecutions conducted by various sectors of the regime.

Until the war, anti-Jewish policy was actually shaped by
several factions. One was the ministerial bureaucracy, made
up of conservatives dedicated to the well-ordered functioning
of the government and supported by ministers like Frick
(Interior) and Schacht (Finance). It played an important part
both in promoting and in curbing anti-Jewish legislation.
The Nazi party, led by Hess, was a second factor, which
was determined to gain control of the state administration
and which persistently incited it to aggravate the situation
of the Jews. Thirdly, Goebbels and Streicher, one the Minister of Propaganda and the Gauleiter of Berlin, the other
the Gauleiter of Franconia and a fanatical anti-Semite, put
their shoulders to the wheel too, as did a good number
of middle- and lower-echelon party members. Himmler, as
head of both the SS and the police, would also play an
expanding role by exploiting his growing independence from
both the state administration and the party. Finally, Hitler,
who had to take his conservative allies into account as well
as the possible reactions of the people and the Churches,
and who was determined to keep the role of arbiter and
decision-maker, recognized by all. He was not, therefore,
the only actor behind anti-Semitic policy, nor even always
the main actor. Was he, however, the determining actor?
We shall answer by retracing the policy pursued during the
peacetime years.

Hitler did not come to power with a dossier full of
anti-Jewish measures tucked under his arm, measures he
would enact according to some preset schedule. There is
no doubt, however, that he had in mind the major lines of
his future action. During the preceding years the Nazi party
had prepared a number of studies and plans. These set out
the minimum goals agreed upon by Nazi leaders, and would

be enacted during the next two years: the exclusion of Jews from public office, a ban on marriages with Germans, and relegation to a status of second-class citizen. Certain plans went even further by providing for the immediate removal of German citizenship from all Jews, opening the way to enforced emigration or expulsion.[1]

During the early months of the regime, a semi-chaotic situation prevailed. Nazi mobs began hunting down their political opponents and sending them to concentration camps. Groups of storm-troopers spread terror through the streets, swooping on Jewish pedestrians, savagely beating them, often stripping them of their money, and sometimes leaving them dead: 45 Jews were killed in this fashion in 1933, and hundreds of others wounded more or less severely. Local branches of the party were also active in organizing boycotts and forcing the resignation of certain public servants. For their part, municipal and regional authorities fired their Jewish employees and harassed Jews under their administration. Confronted by this situation, the ministerial bureaucracy decided to sanction and standardize these practices by passing a law excluding Jews from public office.

In the meantime, these acts of violence and vandalism had stirred world opinion: calls for a boycott of German merchandise were heard in a number of countries. Hitler intervened at this point, entrusting to Goebbels and Streicher the organization of a boycott of Jewish businesses for 1 April. The idea had probably come from party ranks, perhaps from Goebbels himself, who wrote in his diary that the Führer had 'now reached a decision'.[2] Hitler had taken the situation back in hand while satisfying the party activists. At the same time he put pressure on conservatives, urging them to adopt anti-Jewish measures. Finally he was making his intentions known and stressing the importance he placed on the question.[3] His world vision had provided him with an instant interpretation of the call for a boycott of German exports. He revealed it to his Council of Ministers on 14 July 1933: international Jewry was trying to eliminate him; German Jews would suffer the consequences of a boycott aimed at the Reich.[4] Already at a government meeting on 29 March, he had justified his own boycott by declaring that the Jews must understand that a war against Germany would strike them first.[5] Seeing Jews as hostages and objects

of reprisal was a reaction that characterized his behaviour
from the beginning.

The boycott of 1 April only reinforced the hostility of
international opinion: German exports soon felt the consequences. In Germany it worried conservatives such as
Neurath, who was alarmed by its repercussions on foreign
policy, and Hindenburg, who had not supported it but
had not wished to oppose it openly.[6] The Nazi leaders
glimpsed the limits of their freedom of action. They would
encounter them again in connection with the projected law
on public service. This bill barred access to public office
to 'non-Aryans', a bizarre formula that originated in the
administration's difficulty in defining who was Jewish. In
the application decrees, it was established that the law would
affect all persons having at least one grandparent of the
Jewish religion: the indefinable race boiled down to religion.
The conservatives certainly had no objection to the promul-
gation of a discriminatory statute. But they did not support
the Nazi's racist concept: services rendered to the country
should differentiate one Jew from another. Hindenburg took
a stand on this issue by demanding the inclusion of a clause
of exception, notably for Jewish veterans.

Hitler had to yield, ungraciously it seems from the following incident. On 14 July 1933 the government was considering proposed legislation about lawyers, a profession from
which 'non-Aryans' would also be excluded. During the
debate on a possible exception for Jewish veterans, Hitler
intervened with a more draconian viewpoint than the one
provided for in the proposal. The entire Jewish people should
be turned away, he declared, adding that, in the case under
consideration, exception could be made only for Jews who
had seen combat, not for those who had simply been in the
war zone, for example in ordnance or in the military courts.[7]
He could not have more clearly demonstrated his intense
involvement with anti-semitic legislation and his desire for
maximum exclusion.

He had none the less assessed the obstacles to a speedy
settlement of the question. Foreign-policy considerations
were a top priority. On 6 June 1933 he disclosed his plan
of action to Senior officials in the administration, for the
most part also party regulars. He intended to rearm, he
said, while 'outwardly talking ceaselessly about peace and
disarmament.' He would conduct 'a policy of entente, in

order to arrive later at a policy of force'. He alluded to the Soviet Union, which the Jews were supposedly ruining, adding: 'One day we shall come as heirs.' In the meantime the 'new Germany' confronted a league of enemies she must not provoke unnecessarily, since the rest of the world was being manipulated by Jews with 'endless possibilities of exerting influence'. Every measure adopted against the Jews in Germany would resonate among their brothers abroad and in the governments they controlled. It was therefore essential not to 'let ourselves to be drawn into reckless acts'.[8]

Proposed legislation on mixed marriages and citizenship, the drafting of which had begun, was therefore placed on a back burner. But directions had been clearly indicated, and Hitler had played a major role in that. He had shown that he made the 'Jewish question' his personal business, and also that he knew how to tailor his policy to fit the circumstances. In the following years there would be many examples of this calculated and generally moderating approach. In October 1933, for example, he opposed a ruling that the law forbidding party members to buy from Jewish businesses be extended to civil servants.[9]

As well as enacting these early anti-Semitic measures, he also attended to other facets of his racist programme. Thus he imposed on his conservative allies a law requiring the compulsory sterilization of persons with hereditary illnesses; approximately 400,000 Germans were its victims in the following years.[10] In 1937, over the objections of the Minister of Foreign Affairs, he ordered that the measure be extended to a category of persons entirely free of disease. As a result, some 500 young people born of German women and African soldiers of the French occupation army were sterilized.[11]

In 1934 anti-Semitic legislation experienced a slow-down, but action aimed at the Jews did not stop for all that. Numerous pressures were brought to bear on them individually, making their economic survival difficult, especially in rural areas. The ministries, for their part, continued to adopt measures that limited Jewish freedom. Everything moved towards making their lives in Germany impossible. The emigration of all Jews was the long-range goal, and Himmler's offices intended to contribute to its realization. Since it was difficult, because of the world economic crisis, to find host countries, and since there were no directives to the contrary from Hitler, they played the cards of Zionism and Palestine.

The SD (Sicherheitsdienst), the party's intelligence service which, like the security police, the Sipo (Sicherheitspolizei), was under Heydrich's direction, stated the matter clearly in 1934: to encourage the departure of the Jews from Germany, it was necessary to develop in them the consciousness of a separate identity.[12] Zionist organizations therefore received favoured treatment; their interests coincided here with those of a regime only too happy to see the proliferation of Hebrew schools, sporting clubs, and professional retraining courses geared to emigration to Palestine. One of the Nuremberg laws, that concerning 'the sanctity of German blood and honour' which forbade the Jews to display the swastika, expressly authorized them to fly the blue and white Zionist flag stamped with the Star of David. It was in the same spirit of encouraging emigration that an agreement was reached in 1933 with the Jewish Agency; this agreement permitted well-to-do Jews to move a large part of their possessions to Palestine, in exchange for an increase in German exports.[13]

But should they go? Two years after the Nazi rise to power, the situation seemed to have calmed. While most Jewish civil servants, lawyers, and doctors had had to abandon their professions, the rest, the great majority, had not been legally affected in their economic activity. All had watched with relief the return of a semblance of calm and order, and almost all wanted to believe in the tranquillity. After a huge wave of emigration in 1933, departures diminished and re-entries even began to occur. Nazi leaders took a dim view of this, and the Gestapo received the order to send Jews who insisted on returning to concentration camps.

But the machinery of persecution seemed only to stall. In the spring of 1935 it enjoyed a new acceleration at the hands of men like Streicher and Goebbels, irritated by the lull in anti-Semitic legislation. By summer, a situation comparable to that in the regime's first months had developed. Throughout the country there were boycotts of Jewish business as well as terrorist actions, restrictions on access to public buildings and places, and expulsions from associations that still had Jewish members. Goebbels denounced the absence of a law preventing marriages between Jews and Germans. The party called for the identification of Jewish businesses, and criticized the official line that Jews should be allowed to work in peace.[14]

Was this campaign launched or simply encouraged by Hitler? Goebbels noted in his diary on 29 April 1935 that he had discussed 'Jewish arrogance' with Hitler. The Führer had shown himself to be 'very receptive' and had let it be known that changes soon would be made.[15] Judging from this source, Hitler only encouraged the movement. Goebbels, along with Streicher, was probably the initiator of the campaign, which was designed to reactivate anti-Jewish legislation and won an immediate warm welcome from the party rank and file. The ministerial bureaucracy could not stand idly by. Frick and Schacht condemned the unrest and pronounced themselves in favour of a legal and progressive settlement of the 'Jewish question'. They none the less had to announce that laws designed to meet certain express demands were in train. Hitler distanced himself from developments during a great part of this campaign, but probably followed it closely. At a certain point he decided that things had gone too far: in August he barred the party militants from all further unauthorized actions.

When the party congress met in Nuremberg in September, the situation had quietened down, but nothing had been accomplished. Hitler must have judged that the time had come to give a new impetus and to meet, at least partially, his troops' expectations. He therefore abruptly summoned his experts on anti-Jewish policy and asked them to draft laws on citizenship and marriage, which were promptly adopted by the parliament sitting in extraordinary session in Nuremberg. Marriages as well as sexual relations between Jews and Germans would henceforth be banned, and Jews would be given the status of second-class citizen. Hitler presented these laws as responses to the boycott against Germany organized by Jews abroad. He spoke of them as a solution which 'perhaps' would lay the foundations for a peaceful coexistence between Jews and Germans. But, he added, if the Jewish campaign inside and outside Germany persisted, there would be a re-examination of the matter. The situation remained precarious; the lot of Jews in Germany could only worsen.

Hitler had threatened in passing to entrust the 'final solution' of the 'Jewish problem' to the party if the administration continued to drag its feet,[16] thereby encouraging the former and warning the latter. However, he had no intention of aligning himself with either side, as the following events will show. Once the laws were passed there remained the problem of specifying to whom they applied. Cases of persons with four Jewish grandparents were clear-cut. But what about those with one, two, or three Jewish grandparents? The answer had thus far remained unclear, although the party's position had been known for a long time: persons having only one Jewish grandparent would also be considered Jewish. The party refused to admit the existence of 'half-castes', unlike the ministerial bureaucracy, which wanted a narrower definition of persons to be considered Jewish.

A document never before quoted (to my knowledge) offers an extremely interesting insight into Hitler's intentions and, incidentally, into his methods of leadership. On 25 September 1935 a meeting was held under the chairmanship of Walter Gross, the chief of the Nazi party's bureau of racial policy. Gross had assembled the regional leaders of his department to brief them on Hitler's decisions regarding the application of the Nuremberg laws.[17] In his opening remarks Gross recalled that the goal of the Third Reich's policy was the expulsion of Jewish influence 'in the sense of the removal of a foreign body' ('im Sinne der Ausscheidung eines Fremdkörpers'). He continued by severely criticizing Streicher's action: it had led the Führer to intervene 'personally' to announce a decision that required a genuine change of attitude from the party. Hitler had, in effect, pronounced in favour of recognizing the category of 'half-caste', in which he placed the half-Jews. Pondering the fate of these persons, he had mentioned three possible solutions: '(1) expulsion or emigration under state pressure, (2) sterilization, (3) assimilation.' His policy being to choose the lesser of two evils, he had decided that the 'half-caste' question should be settled through assimilation over the next few generations.

Hitler had thus come out against the party point of view. The justification he gave is interesting. His goal was to make Germany powerful and prepared to strike ('schlagkräftig') so that, in the trials to come, she would be capable of shaping her own destiny. Everything that could obstruct this goal must be swept aside; for his part, he did not wish to create a caste of people uncertain of its allegiance. Gross attributed another motive to him, of an economic nature, Schacht having pointed out that a stricter regulation might damage German exports. Hitler had stressed, in other words, that the realities must be taken into account: since he had decided on the rearmament and military build-up of the country, 'everything else must be subordinated to this goal'.

He had made it known, furthermore, that he desired an end to the boycott movement. Work opportunities must be opened to Jews so that they did not wind up on public assistance; their exclusion from the economy, insisted on by the party, was therefore postponed. He wished, moreover, that Zionism not be encouraged, but also that there be a 'more vigorous emigration' on the part of the Jews. Gross reported, finally, 'on the Führer's specific order', that these new decisions – the one concerning 'half-castes' in particular – were not just 'a tactical manœuvre': they signified a fundamental reorientation.

It is difficult to deny, on the strength of this document, that Hitler had a clear vision of his objective, the steps that would lead to it, and the priorities to be considered. The departure of all Jews from Germany was the objective. Putting an end to their economic activity would be the next big step, and he saw its consequences: their impoverishment, and the burden that would weigh on the Reich. He had also indicated what his priority was: that anti-Jewish policy be pursued in terms of the possibilities, taking care not to obstruct the main goal, the restoration of national power. If he had chosen the most moderate solution *vis-à-vis* the half-castes, it was because he was aware of the repercussions another solution might have on the German population, especially on the next of kin of the persons involved. But it was also because he sensed that his position was sufficiently secure: periods of success did not incline him toward extreme solutions.

The same document confirms this *a contrario* by reporting another statement, extremely enlightening for our purposes. Still according to Gross, immediately after having announced that he was in favour of the assimilation of half-castes, Hitler had added that 'in the event of a war on all fronts, he would be "ready for all the consequences"*' ('An dieser Stelle erklärt er noch, dass er im Falle eines Krieges auf allen Fronten"bereit zu allen Konsequenzen" sei" '). In other words, he would go back on his decision in the event of finding himself in a difficult or hopeless situation; and

* The phrase used by Hitler implies the idea of being 'prepared to go to any extreme'.

go back on it by adopting another policy toward Jewish
half-castes, a policy which would evidently apply all the
more to full Jews. 'In the event of a war on all fronts', he
would take certain unspecified steps which, to judge from
the threatening phrase quoted by Gross, would clearly be
radical.

The matter might seem to have been settled. But nothing
of the sort was true, and what happened next sheds light
on Hitler's style of leadership. On 29 September, a few days
after the meeting presided over by Gross, Hitler was to communicate his position to the highest party officials. However,
instead of reporting the decision he had indicated to Gross,
even though his remarks, on the whole, seemed headed in
that direction (and showed, incidentally, a knowledge of the
dossier that impressed the chargé for Jewish affairs at the
Ministry of the Interior), he closed by saying that a few points
remained to be clarified and that he would leave it up to the
Party and the Ministry of the Interior to settle them.[18]

A fight promptly broke out between the representatives
of these two institutions, a fight that was both sordid
and dramatic in that it decided the fate of tens of thousands
of people. While the Interior Ministry proposed a solution
close to the one favoured by Hitler, the party, after having had to give up its category of quarter-Jews (a single
Jewish grandparent), insisted that at least the half-Jews
be considered as full Jews. It further demanded obligatory
divorce for existing mixed marriages, and even sterilization
in questionable cases. An inter-ministerial meeting, called for
5 November to settle the matter in Hitler's presence, was
cancelled by him. On 14 November he finally signed an order
that essentially represented the Interior Ministry's point of
view: half-Jews would be counted as Germans, unless they
were married to a Jew or were of the Jewish religion.[19]

If Hitler postponed the announcement of his decision on
29 September, it was probably because he knew it would
displease high party officials. Goebbels was one of those
pressuring him to take a harder line. On 1 October he noted,
after a conversation about the Jewish question, 'We discussed
it at length, but the Führer is still undecided.' On 7 November
he wrote that the Führer now wanted a resolution; but this
clearly would not be in line with what Goebbels had hoped:
a compromise would be necessary, he added with regret. On
15 November he indicated that the final decision had been

made. It was not what he had wanted, but he was relieved nevertheless: 'In God's name, at last peace comes.'[20]

Hitler's behaviour was characteristic. He had developed a technique of postponing decisions until, after lengthy discussions, the parties were ready to welcome his intervention with relief. In this case we can see that, far from having been led to sanction increasingly radical decisions emerging from the competition between the regime's different factions, he had, through his temporizing tactics, induced his lieutenants to accept a point of view more moderate than their own. Hitler dominated the situation: he meant to be the master of the party as well as of the bureaucracy, and to be the prisoner of no one. In Nuremberg he had issued a warning to the bureaucracy, which did not keep him from promptly approving the moderate solution it proposed. As for the party, after offering encouragement, he gave it to understand that he alone decided the pace and scope of anti-Jewish policy.[21]

Anti-Jewish policy had a relatively limited place in Hitler's preoccupations at the time. The main thrust of his effort was to regain freedom of action in Europe, and to rebuild a military force that would permit him to act when the time came. Success crowned him, it must be said, with incredible constancy. After having reinstated compulsory military service in 1935, he concluded a naval accord with Great Britain in June which split his enemies' front and appeared to advance his plans for an alliance with London. Shortly afterwards, the war in Ethiopia played into his hands by bringing Italy closer. In March 1936, seizing the opportunity, he sent troops into the demilitarized zone of the Rhineland, and lost no time building fortifications to protect his rear when the day came to move against Austria, Czechoslovakia, or Poland.

Goebbels was very much in favour at the time, and his diaries offer many glimpses of the dreams and ambitions of Hitler's foreign policy. In them we find the great themes established in the 1920s: the alliance with England, the conquest of Lebensraum to the East, the acquisition of hegemony in Europe, and the dissolution of the Peace of Westphalia.[22] We find the same all-or-nothing state of mind: in the coming struggle, Germany would be victorious or would cease to exist.[23] But anti-Jewish policy is mentioned only infrequently, either measures contemplated or ultimate objectives. It was in November 1937 that this theme was first the subject of a long conversation. Goebbels noted that the Führer was firmly resolved to make the Jews leave not only Germany but also all of Europe.[24] It was the first indication of an intention that would be powerfully articulated in the years to come, and would gather strength with each success.

For the time being, the objective on which party leaders and state officials set their sights was the departure of the Jews from Germany. It was even understood that emigration could eventually be achieved 'through coercion'.[25] But it was also typical of the Nazi mentality that, when it came to the Jews, every solution immediately presented a new problem. The Jews would have to leave Germany, but would their departure not be damaging to the Reich's interests? The question of emigration to Palestine, in particular, stirred up acrimonious debate between the different party and state services. Should the departure of the Jews for any destination be encouraged, or should the birth of a Jewish nation in Palestine be obstructed? Hitler himself wrestled with this sort of dilemma, which sprang from his obsessive need to cover every eventuality; but he was no less determined that the Jews must go. At the beginning of 1938, he formally declared that he favoured the stimulation of emigration 'by every possible means' – in other words, including emigration to Palestine.[26]

But while he wanted the Jews to leave, he also wanted to use them as hostages. What galvanized him emotionally, still and always, was the prospect of exploiting them as objects of reprisal. On 4 February 1936 a young Jew, David Frankfurter, assassinated Gustloff, the official responsible for German Nazis living in Switzerland. In view of the imminent start of the Winter Olympic Games, and in view also of the preparations being made for the remilitarization of the Rhineland, Hitler ordered the party to refrain from taking any action. As Hess emphasized in the circular he dispatched to restrain his troops: 'Today, as yesterday, it is the Führer alone who decides, in each individual case, what policy to pursue.'[27] However, it had cost Hitler dearly to renounce immediate revenge.

A few months later, in a memorandum he was drafting to determine the goals of rearmament, he called in passing for the enactment of a law that would hold all Jews responsible for crimes committed by one of them against the economy or against the German people; he had in mind the Gustloff affair. The bureaucracy reacted to this demand in a manner that demonstrates the limits of Hitler's power at the time. The Minister of Justice let it be known, in effect, that the concept of collective reprisals went against the law, and suggested that a substitute solution be sought in the form of a fiscal measure. Hitler retreated to the idea of a special tax whose amount would be fixed each year, and which would be used to encourage the emigration of Jews. Most interestingly, he ordered that the finalization of this tax be expedited so that it could be announced at the end of the trial of Gustloff's murderer.[28]

He had not lost sight of the Gustloff affair: the idea of reprisals was still uppermost in his mind. The special tax was supposed to encourage emigration, but it is obvious that Hitler particularly relished its retaliatory value. The relationship between a policy of removal and a policy of reprisal, not to mention a policy of revenge absent from the agenda in those halcyon times, had been, to all intents and purposes, strained if not contradictory from the start, as we have seen. In practice, the effects became clear. If Hitler had energetically supported emigration from the beginning, he would have achieved better results. But he also needed to satisfy his deepest inclination, which was vindictive. Torn between these two opposing inclinations, he was, by his ambivalence, facilitating the faltering course of his regime's anti-Jewish policy.

The year 1938 constituted a turning-point in several respects. To the immense satisfaction of the party faithful, the expulsion of the Jews from the economy, called 'aryanization' in Nazi jargon, became the order of the day, and a vigorous, centralized emigration policy followed in its wake. But the persecution also took new forms, with the introduction of more brutal methods designed to accelerate the Jews' departure. The annexation of Austria, then the triumphal occupation of the Sudetenland, conceded by the Western powers at Munich, somewhat lessened the concern about international repercussions which until then had served as a curb.

It was in Austria, immediately after the annexation, that the hardening of anti-Jewish activity first crystallized. Here, as it would later in other annexed territories, the Nazi regime enforced a harsher policy than it did in the old

Reich, the period of upheaval offering an opportunity to create *faits accomplis* which could then be extended to the Reich as a whole. Immediately after the annexation an atmosphere of pogrom descended on Vienna, where the heavy concentration of Jews was accompanied by an old anti-Semitic tradition. The spectacle of groups of people forced to humiliate themselves before a jeering crowd is one of the most shameful scenes in a century that did not stint on such sights. Countless acts of sadistic brutality were also committed, and hundreds of apartments looted. On the night of 13 March it was the turn of the police to help themselves to the possessions of Austrian Jews; on Hitler's orders, the most beautiful objects were to be shipped back to Berlin.[29]

It was in Vienna, on 26 March 1938, that Goering, head of the Four-Year Plan and master of the German economy, first made aryanization the order of the day, specifying that it was to be 'carried out thoughtfully and methodically'.[30] But to no avail: in the following months aryanization, which was still in principle 'voluntary', took the form, in Austria, of a gigantic extortion. The application of every sort of pressure forced many Jews to liquidate their possessions at rock-bottom prices and to emigrate. Nazi action even went so far as to employ, for the first time, a direct means of expulsion. At the end of March, the police drove the Jews of Burgenland across the Hungarian frontier with only such belongings as they were able to carry.[31]

It was also in Vienna that the emigration system conceived by Eichmann, one of the experts in the SD on the Jewish question, was inaugurated. Eichmann concentrated all the various service personnel specializing in emigration matters in one building: Jews walked out of it with a visa and little else left in their pockets. Since most countries asked for a guarantee in foreign currency before issuing a visa, Eichmann forced rich Jews to deposit a portion of their money to finance the departure of poor Jews. This was, in effect, a double confiscation, since the foreign currency was provided from abroad by Jewish relief organizations and Eichmann resold it at an inflated exchange rate.

Meanwhile, in the old Reich, aryanization was taking its place on the agenda. The previous autumn, a series of laws had been passed to limit the economic activity of Jews. In April 1938 they were obliged to declare their total assets. But uncertainty still reigned over which course to pursue:

coercion by decree or inducement by fiscal legislation. In April, Hitler revived the idea of a special tax, which had until then gone no further; such a tax with a sliding scale, he repeated, would allow him to penalize Jews in cases where they acted as 'enemies of the people'.[32] Obviously he did not envision a rapid aryanization and the prompt departure of the Jews from Germany.

Once again the project would be shelved. The ministerial bureaucracy instead began to explore the means of achieving aryanization by coercion. In June, a memorandum from the Minister of the Interior proposed the first overall plan, under which Jews would be obliged to sell their businesses in return for compensation in the form of state bonds. The Minister of the Economy, as well as Schacht in his role as President of the Bank of the Reich, immediately raised objections. They feared the economic repercussions of immediate aryanization, not to mention the risk of the proletarianization of the Jews and the ensuing burden on public assistance. Their preference was for an aryanization to be effected over several years. On 14 October, at an inter-ministerial meeting under Goering's chairmanship, the agreement in principle to exclude Jews from economic life was reaffirmed, but no concrete advances were made. Besides, the eventual fate of the Jews was starting to seem like a problem. Goering refused to sacrifice the Reich's scant foreign currencies to permit them to leave with what remained of their assets, and considered concentrating them in ghettos and obliging them to perform public service.[33]

As the aryanization project limped slowly through the bureaucratic mazes, fever flared up anew among party members at the end of the spring of 1938. Once more, Goebbels seized the initiative, bending his efforts towards a radical goal. This time he intended to expel the Jews from Berlin. In preference to legal processes, he chose the path of police chicanery.[34] The results were not what he had anticipated. Against his instructions, excesses occurred in the form of lootings and other acts of violence. To faciliate the operation, the police arrested some 1,500 Jews who had police records or had committed misdemeanours. There was, however, one consolation for Goebbels. On 25 July, after a meeting with Hitler, he noted in his diaries that the Führer had approved his Berlin action, and that criticism in the foreign press was of little importance: the essential was that the Jews be driven out; in ten years they must be gone from Germany. But 'for the present we still want to keep the Jews here as security,'[35] he wrote, making the split between the two faces of Hitler's attitude glaringly obvious.

By the summer of 1938, the top echelons of the regime were agreed that anti-Jewish policy must enter a new stage. But, as we have seen, nothing concrete had been decided, and Hitler himself was in no hurry. In fact, other problems vied for his attention: the Czechoslovakian crisis loomed large on the horizon. After the triumph in Munich, he found himself burdened with additional Jews he would try to get rid of as best he could. To this end he asked von Ribbentrop to look into the possibility of expelling the 27,000 Czechoslovakian Jews living in Vienna. As for the Jewish residents of the recently annexed Sudetenland, they were summarily ousted by the Gestapo and sent to Czechoslovakia, which turned them away. After wandering pitifully in this no man's land, they were eventually taken in by various other countries.

All this was a rehearsal in miniature for what would happen with the Polish Jews. The policy of compulsory emigration pursued by the Reich in Austria had led neighbouring countries, where the tide of anti-Semitism was rising, to close their frontiers. But Poland did not stop there. In early October she announced that the passports of her nationals living abroad must be stamped with a new visa by the end of the month; this visa could be denied to persons who had resided outside Poland for more than five years. The goal of this ruling was to prevent Germany from sending her Jewish residents of Polish nationality back to their homeland. It presented Nazi authorities with the prospect of inheriting several tens of thousands of stateless persons who would then have difficulty in emigrating. They therefore decided to take extreme measures. Shortly before the end of the month, 15,000–20,000 Polish Jews were arrested by the Gestapo and escorted to the frontier in a state of utter destitution. The Polish authorities refused to accept them, and it was only at the end of lengthy negotiations that a compromise agreement was reached in which Germany finally succeeded in ridding herself of most of these 'undesirables'.[36]

A few days later, on 7 November, a young Polish Jew named Herschel Grynszpan, whose family had just been deported, assaulted a German diplomat in Paris. The victim died of his wounds two days later. Nazi leaders learned of his death as they gathered in Munich for their annual celebration of the 1923 Putsch. After talking with Hitler, Goebbels gave a speech in which he made it known that this aggression by Jews against the Reich would be met with a reign of terror. That same night the most brutal pogrom Western Europe had known in centuries was unleashed, leaving nearly 100 dead and causing the destruction of thousands of homes and hundreds of synagogues. The police arrested some 30,000 well-to-do Jews and sent them to concentration camps; they were released during the following weeks in exchange for written promises to leave the country immediately.

Uncertainty persists about the exact orders Hitler gave Goebbels. According to the results of an inquiry conducted by the Nazi party tribunal, it seems that he authorized the holding of spontaneous demonstrations; the party was neither to initiate nor to lead them. In his speech, however, Goebbels made it clear that the party's role was to organize them behind the scenes.[37] While Hitler could only have endorsed the concept of exacting reprisals, he seems to have been surprised by the extent of the destruction; soon he would be able to gauge its impact. The German people had disapproved of the pogrom; foreign opinion strongly condemned it; and even some Nazi leaders, Goering and Himmler at their head, were critical. In each case Hitler covered for Goebbels, who did not derive the hoped-for benefits from the affair. His relationship with the Führer, which was becoming strained, deteriorated even more in the next two or three years. Hitler, however, had learned his lesson. There would be no further public violence against the Jews in Germany. At the outbreak of war, as well as in September 1941, when the wearing of the yellow star was imposed, he issued very strict orders to forestall any incident.

In the wake of 'Kristallnacht', settling the 'Jewish problem' could no longer be put off. On 12 November another inter-ministerial meeting took place under the chairmanship of Goering, who announced that, in accordance with the mandate the Führer had just given him, the question must 'now be addressed in a centralized fashion and resolved one way or another'.[38] The summary he gave of the developments of the preceding months emphasized the lack of coherence and continuity which had, in effect, characterized the regime's policy. 'Grand designs' had been conceived to aryanize the economy, but they had only been half-heartedly executed. Then demonstrations had broken out in Berlin and it had been a question of making critical decisions; once again, nothing had happened. Finally the murder in Paris had taken place, with its infamous consequences, 'and now something must be done!'

First Goering described the decisions that had been made for settling the damages caused by 'Kristallnacht'. Insurance companies would have to honour policies contracted with Jews, but the compensation monies would go to the state. Jews would nevertheless be obliged to make repairs to their property at their own expense. An exceptional tax of one thousand million Reichsmarks would furthermore be imposed upon them. The state would reap all the profit from the affair; the money would go to rearmament. Then Goering announced that henceforth Jews would be excluded from the economy; they would be compensated with debentures on which they would have to live. Only one problem remained which did not seem to have preoccupied Goering, but which Heydrich did not fail to raise: that of the departure of the Jews from Germany, particularly of the 'rabble' who did not have the money to emigrate.

Heydrich explained to the assembly the procedure followed in Austria which had resulted in the emigration of 50,000 Jews as opposed to 19,000 in Germany during the same period. Goering obviously was not *au courant* with Eichmann's system; he was afraid it might cost the Reich precious foreign currency. Heydrich's response reassured him: the Jews would cost only the foreign currency allocated to them – which amounted to stripping them of as much as possible. Goering approved Heydrich's proposal to create a centre for emigration in Germany modelled on the the one in Vienna; it would, according to Heydrich, assure the departure of all Jews from Germany in eight to ten years.

The decisions reached at the 12 November meeting were approved by Hitler, as Goering announced on 5 December during a meeting of the Gauleiters. Aryanization would first affect businesses, then real estate property. Jews could still make their purchases in German stores. Finally, regarding emigration, the departure of the poorest Jews must be arranged first. For those who remained, Hitler had rejected the wearing of a badge, proposed by Heydrich.[39] He had justified his decision by explaining that a distinctive insignia might expose the Jews to new acts of violence and make their shopping for provisions difficult.[40]

He had not ruled on a number of other proposals made by Goebbels and Heydrich, which aimed at excluding Jews from social life and separating them from Germans. To all appearances, Goering hounded him until, at the end of December, he got an answer. Hitler declared himself against the creation of ghettos: Jews were to be assembled gradually in separate apartment buildings. They would henceforth be denied the use of dining cars and sleeping cars on trains; but access to public transportation and public places would remain open. Licensed Jewish civil servants would continue to receive their pensions. Finally, Jewish social assistance would continue its activity so as to keep Jews from becoming charges of the state. Once again Hitler had ruled from on high, rejecting the radical proposals of Goebbels and Heydrich even though they aimed at goals he cherished.[41]

'Kristallnacht' had given a powerful impetus to anti-Jewish policy. The aryanization of the economy was settled and was to be achieved in the following months. The emigration of Jews received serious attention for the first time; it was to be handled in a rigorous, centralized fashion. On 24 January 1939 Goering gave Heydrich the order to establish a centre for Jewish emigration similar to the one in Vienna, and to run it so as to make Germany 'judenfrei', 'free of Jews'. It was a triumph for Heydrich, who began to consolidate the execution of the regime's anti-Jewish policy in his own hands. During the next two years, he would dedicate himself to furthering Jewish emigration by any means, including encouraging the illegal emigration to Palestine organized by the Zionists.

Hitler had resolved to make the departure of the Jews an immediate political objective. He did this at a time when emigration had become more difficult than ever, particularly since the German Jews were destined to lose the greater part of their resources. Nevertheless, he pursued his goal with undeniable determination. At the beginning of 1939 he even authorized Schacht to find, with the other Western nations, a way to facilitate emigration by allowing Jews to transfer their assets abroad. The negotiation was carried on by a representative of Goering and resulted in an accord whose implementation was cut short by the outbreak of war.[42] While

130,000 Jews had emigrated from Germany from 1933 to 1937, almost 40,000 of them to Palestine, 118,000 more left in 1938 and 1939 despite far more difficult conditions. To this must be added the emigration of Austrian Jews after the Anschluss: from May 1938 to September 1939, slightly more than 100,000 persons departed.[43]

While he was 'freeing' Germany from Jews, Hitler was also trying to raise the question to a European level. He had told Goebbels in November 1937 that some day the Jews would also have to leave Europe. He repeated this on 24 November 1938, to Pirow, the South African Minister of Defence and Economy: 'some day, the Jews will disappear from Europe.'[44] He had always stressed that the question was not, in his eyes, a purely German one. After the autumn of 1938, he made it a concern of international politics. It was a means among others of initiating or strengthening political and diplomatic ties. But it was also a means of making the departure of Germany's Jews acceptable to himself. In the future they would be less and less useful as hostages; and he now felt sufficiently sure of his power to do without them. But he could not forego the search for a larger solution that would render harmless as many European Jews as possible.

By 20 September he had already told the Polish ambassador, Lipski, that he hoped to settle the Jewish question by mutual agreement with other countries like Poland, Hungary, and perhaps Romania, and that he was thinking of shipping the Jews to a colony. Lipski replied that if he, Hitler, could find a solution to the problem, the Poles would build a monument in his honour in Warsaw.[45] Was Hitler at this point envisioning a solution like Madagascar? It seems so, to judge by Goering's remarks at the 12 November meeting: on 9 November Hitler had told him of his intention to approach other countries about settling the Jewish question on an international level; he had also mentioned Madagascar. From then on, the deportation of European Jews to a distant territory was discussed in high Nazi circles. On 12 November Goering suggested another possibility: rich Jews could buy land in America or Canada and settle their racial brothers there.

By bringing the question to the international community, Hitler entered propitious ground. Romania and Poland had let it be known that they, too, would like to find a place to settle their Jews. Even Roosevelt had come out in favour of a Jewish settlement in Angola.[46] In January 1939 Hitler discussed the problem at length during meetings with some Eastern European leaders. Clearly, he was seeking to persuade other countries to follow his example or rally to his cause. As he had told Pirow, he was exporting his anti-Semitism. On 5 January he indicated to the Polish Minister of Foreign Affairs, Beck, that he favoured settling the Jews in a distant land: he added that he himself might have placed an African territory at their disposition if the Western powers had had a better understanding of his colonial claims.[47]

He also pressured the countries under his influence to take up the battle against the Jews by following the German example. On 21 January he told the Czech Minister of Foreign Affairs, Chvalkovsky, that the Jews would be 'annihilated' in the Reich: they had done the same to Germany on 9 November 1918; that day would be avenged. It was a question here of the annihilation of the Jews as a community living in Germany, not of their physical extermination. In effect, Hitler suggested to the Minister that the anti-Semitic countries deport their Jews to any place on earth and notify the Anglo-Saxon countries, who were always mouthing humanitarian principles, to take care of them or have their deaths on their consciences.[48] We shall come across this idea later: Hitler had no intention of making any sacrifices whatsoever for the Jews; the ideal would have been to ship them out of Europe without having to worry about their fate or, more importantly, their upkeep.

The speech he gave before the Reichstag on 30 January 1939 followed the campaign line pursued since the previous autumn.[49] The Jews, he declared, were the enemies of national socialism throughout the entire world. No external force could influence the settlement of this problem in Germany: the Jews would have to leave the country where they had made themselves so much at home. But this alone would not solve the 'Jewish problem'. It was a European problem, and Europe would not be able to rest until it was settled. Actually, he added, this might be a common ground for countries which, at the moment, held diverging viewpoints. In any case, the world had enough open space left to colonize, and it was time for the Jews to break away from their lives as parasites. They, too, would have to work with their hands like other people; otherwise, sooner or later, they would risk undergoing 'a crisis of unimaginable proportions.'

He continued by saying that he had often in the past been a prophet, and that people had laughed at his prophecies. The Jews, in particular, had laughed when he announced that one day he would be in power, and that then he would resolve 'among many other problems, the Jewish problem as well.' He now wished to make another prophecy: if international Jewry, in and outside Europe, once again forced the nations into a world war, the result would not be the Bolshevization of the earth and victory for the Jews, but the annihilation of the Jewish race in Europe.[50]

There is no possible doubt about the significance of this threat: Hitler had in mind the physical extermination of the Jews. Indeed, he had just evoked another solution, their resettlement in a distant land. So his threat of extermination was conditional: it would be carried out in the event of a world war, i.e. in a situation that meant the endangering, if not the total failure, of his plan. Things might go badly for him in the end; but the European Jews – in other words, the majority of the Jewish people – would pay the price early on: they would not be around to savour his defeat and bask in their victory. It is significant that in this speech he attacked United States policy; in his prophecy he meant American Jews when speaking of Jews 'outside Europe'. The precedent of 1914–18 was still vividly, obsessively present in his mind: a war would not be a world war without the participation of the United States.[51]

Hitler's Jewish policy at the beginning of 1939 thus consisted of several elements. The Jewish problem was in the process of being solved in Germany through compulsory emigration. At the same time, the question had been expanded to a European scale and a solution proposed: the resettlement of European Jews in a distant territory, either through a concerted action or through a unilateral action by Nazi Germany if she were in a position to carry it out. The solution of a Jewish reservation emerged then clearly: it was also expounded during that same period by Rosenberg, and evoked in a circular from the Minister of Foreign Affairs.[52] All this pre-dates by many months the great German victories and the establishment of Nazi hegemony over Europe. And there was one last element: the hypothesis of failure and the announcement of extermination.

Hitler brought his intention out into the open. As he had first done at the Congress of Nuremberg in 1936, he presented himself as a prophet. Success had reinforced his conviction of having a historic mission. At the same time, the spectre of failure never left him: he knew that the time of trial had just begun. By verbalizing his innermost purpose, he also exalted, and empowered, himself. Finally, he issued a warning to the enemy: the Jews of the whole world had been warned; all they had to do now was not to stand in the way of the Reich's triumphant advance. In his 1939 speech, as in his statements to Gross in the autumn of 1935, the announcement of a 'moderate' solution immediately elicited a declaration of revenge in the event of failure.

In six years the Nazi regime had come a long way in its anti-Jewish policy, even if it had done so in a rather erratic fashion. As we have seen, Hitler dominated the situation; he lacked neither goals nor decision-making power. But his conduct was quite different when he dealt with anti-Jewish policy as opposed to foreign policy. With the latter, he displayed a strong presence and a persistent leadership in the service of clearly defined goals; with the former, a sustained attention, a clear general direction, but a somewhat wavering leadership that encouraged initiatives from his lieutenants and yielded a faltering progress in which the action in the streets was a driving force.

Certainly Hitler had to take into account objective pressures, external and internal, in formulating his anti-Jewish policy; but the same was true of his foreign policy. The reason for his behaviour lies, rather, in the priority he had placed on the restoration of national leadership and, above all, in his inner conflict, which gave his lieutenants a chance to join the fray. After the seizure of power, the fight against the Jews remained the party's only battleground; it mobilized the troops and gave a chance to vent their anti-Semitic feelings, prolong their days of activism, and satisfy their appetites. In a certain way, then, the party urged Hitler on: in the direction he himself wanted to go, but probably at a slower pace. For, while he advocated a Germany free of Jews, he also wanted to keep them around as potential hostages for a while. In the end, however, he opted for compulsory emigration; with his power assured, he could do without such pawns in Germany. But it is significant that he then immediately set out in search of an international solution; and that he also publicly voiced his innermost determination. The Jews might leave Germany, but he still would not feel he had evened the score in his struggle against them.

3

The Quest for a Territorial Solution, 1939–1941

Everything had gone admirably for Hitler thus far. He had consolidated his dictatorship, rearmed Germany, and liberated her from most of the shackles imposed at Versailles. Nevertheless, in 1939 he found himself in a position that was the exact opposite of what he had wished. When he invaded Poland on 1 September, he was the ally of the USSR and at war with France and Great Britain. Far from agreeing to divide the world as he had offered, Great Britain had ultimately thrown all her weight against him. Even though his ideal of a succession of localized blitzkriegs had proved flawed, he had the consolation of having averted a war on two fronts, thanks to the neutrality the Soviet Union granted him in return for a new division of Poland and the transfer of the Baltic states into its sphere of influence.

The annihilation of Poland in a few weeks freed him from all danger on his eastern flank, and allowed him to concentrate on preparing for the war in the West. The blitzkriegs of the following spring, from the occupation of Norway to the spectacular defeat of France, would leave him master of the Continent. But, as he soon realized, it was a hollow victory so long as England was resolved to continue the war, the United States, although largely isolationist, determined to aid her materially, and the Soviet Union, finally, still a potential enemy.

In the autumn of 1939, the most astounding successes were yet to come. But Hitler had no need of further victories before tackling some of the more murderous points in his racist ideology. The Nazi war did not become a racist war in June 1941: it had been one since 1 September 1939. And the Jews were not its first victims: the first extermination measures targeting entire groups struck down Germans and Poles.

The German victims were those persons confined to asylums or homes by birth defects or crippling diseases. Hitler, in *Mein Kampf*, had made abundantly clear what he thought of these 'defectives' whose existence testified to the degeneracy of the race, and who were kept alive at great cost by a criminal humanitarianism. It was difficult for him to take care of this 'problem' during his first years in power; but the intention to do so remained. By 1938 the first steps had been taken, although the operation did not get into full swing until the outbreak of war. Solicited by a couple asking him to allow the death of their incurable child, Hitler gave his consent. He then decided that the same fate should be inflicted on all deformed or abnormal newborns. On 18 August 1939, a directive from the Minister of the Interior required all doctors and midwives in the Reich to report infants suffering from a deformity. Placed in special wards, they were killed by injection or starvation.

In the early autumn of 1939, Hitler decided to put an end also to 'the shameful lives of the mentally ill'. A corresponding order was first issued verbally, then during the month of October in the form of a letter pre-dated 1 September 1939. Hitler did not entrust the execution of this project, improperly called 'euthanasia', to Himmler, but to one of his secretariats, the Führer's chancellery, whose job in principle was to process requests from private citizens. It was through this channel that the couple's petition mentioned above had first reached him; it was typical of his style to parcel out missions among the faithful.

The Führer's chancellery, in the greatest secrecy, perfected an organization which later would serve in the extermination of the Jews. A list was drawn up defining the spectrum of victims from schizophrenics, epileptics, and incurable paralytics to the criminally insane. There was one ground for exemption – the ability to work – but it was not valid for criminals, or for Jews after the summer of 1940: at a time when the Nazis sought to expel the Jewish population from the Reich by every available means, they had no intention of supporting persons whose state of health made departure impossible. To transport the designated persons, an organization was created whose vehicles linked asylums with six 'euthanasia' institutes set up across the Reich.

The problem of how to kill these persons still remained. After some trial and error, a uniform procedure was adopted which consisted of undressing the victims, or making them undress, and leading them into a room rigged with dummy showers where they were gassed with tanks of carbon monoxide. After the removal of their gold teeth, the corpses were burned in a crematory oven. A death certificate was sent to the families at the end of a complicated cover-up especially designed to avoid the simultaneous announcement of several deaths in the same locality. In a little under two years, the project claimed more than 70,000 victims. Even though the personnel involved were committed to keeping the operations secret, a mounting wave of protests, notably from churches, ensued; and Hitler suspended the operation in August 1941.[1]

Immediately after the outbreak of war, as he was ordering the 'German body' to be cleansed of creatures 'unworthy of life', Hitler set out to put in place in Poland the foreign plank of his racist platform. Several months before the war started, he had indicated the goals he meant to pursue: the annexation and Germanization of at least a part of Poland, and the destruction of the Polish nation. He remained faithful to the concepts expressed in the 1920s: a territory could only be Germanized by the expulsion of its natives and its colonization by Germans. In November 1937, speaking of the coming conquests of Austria and Czechoslovakia, he had mentioned the expulsion of some 3 million persons from these two countries.[2] But Poland was meant to disappear not only as a sovereign state: she was to vanish as a nation. The goal was 'the elimination of the vital forces' of the country by methods of the 'utmost stringency'.

Poles were doomed to a fate as illiterate and unskilled labourers who would supply the Reich with the manpower it needed. It was therefore necessary to deprive them of a national conscience which, in the Hitlerian vision, was nurtured by the influence of the elite. The suppression of the secondary and higher education systems would contribute significantly to this. But the goal would also be attained by the extermination, pure and simple, of the Polish intelligentsia, of all those who, by reason of their education or social position, could keep the national identity alive.[3]

The mission was entrusted to Himmler who, in September, created the Reich Security Central Office, the RSHA, by combining under Heydrich's direction the security police,

the state organ incorporating the Gestapo, and the SD, a
party organ. Heydrich organized Einsatzgruppen, or 'intervention groups', as he had already done during the invasions
of Austria, the Sudetenland, and then the remainder of
Czechoslovakia. Following on the heels of the Wehrmacht,
these groups had as their mission to secure persons hostile
to the Reich, to impound relevant records, and in general to
combat the ideological enemies of Nazism. But their action
in Poland went beyond anything that had been done in the
past. Armed with lists prepared in advance, Heydrich's men
imprisoned and shot thousands of members of the Polish
elite. These massacres provoked serious tensions with the
army, whose protests put an end to the endeavour.[4]

The Jews were not marked for the death that awaited the
mentally ill and, in part, the Polish elite. Their lot was not
enviable, however. In the wake of the German invasion,
they were the target of countless acts of brutality and
the victims of numerous summary executions carried out
by the Einsatzgruppen. It is estimated that of the some
16,000 civilians executed in the six weeks following the
German attack, at least 5,000 were Jewish.[5] There was no
question of an extermination programme, however, even
though the Nazi regime had extended its control over 2
million additional Jews. On the other hand, while each new
conquest inevitably made the 'Jewish problem' more difficult
to resolve, the acquisition of half of Poland provided a means
of settling it at least temporarily by achieving the goal set
by Rosenberg early in the year, a goal that perfectly fitted
Hitler's vision – that of a Jewish reservation. In the coming
months, the regime's policy was directed towards this end
with dedication, but with very meagre results.

On 14 September 1939 Heydrich announced to his department heads that Himmler was going to submit certain
proposals to Hitler which he alone could rule on, on account
of their possible international repercussions. One week later,
before the same audience augmented by the leaders of the
Einsatzgruppen, he articulated Hitler's views on the future
of Poland. These included the annexation of Western Poland
and the creation of a 'foreign-language' territory with Cracow
as its capital – the future General Government, in which
all Poles would be concentrated, along with all the Jews
and gypsies still resident in the Reich. Regarding the Jews,

Heydrich announced (clearly referring to the fate of the proposals submitted by Himmler) that their deportation to the 'foreign-language' territory as well as their expulsion beyond the German–Soviet demarcation line had been approved by Hitler; the operation was to be accomplished in the space of a year.[6]

Heydrich at once grasped the steps to be taken. Polish Jews must be concentrated as quickly as possible in cities where they could easily be controlled for the moment and subsequently readily deported – in freight cars, as he made a point of specifying. That same day he sent written instructions to the heads of the Einsatzgruppen 'once again' drawing attention to the fact that the 'overall measures programmed (in other words, the final goal) must be kept strictly secret'.[7]

Many historians have wanted to see in this 'final goal' that must be kept secret an allusion to an extermination plan.[8] In reality, the goal being pursued was the concentration of Jews in a reservation. As the same directive stipulated, it was not necessary to regroup in cities Jews living in the region between Cracow, the northern border of Czechoslovakia, and the German–Soviet demarcation line – a stipulation that only made sense if it was understood that this region would become a Jewish reservation. After the final positioning of the demarcation line with the USSR, it was the region a little to the north, around Lublin, that was set aside to become what Heydrich, on 29 September, termed the 'ghetto of the Reich'.[9] As for the secrecy, if Heydrich was so insistent about it, it was probably for diplomatic and security reasons: it was a question of not triggering premature objections from the outside world or alarming the Jews.[10]

On 29 September 1939 Hitler personally revealed his intentions to Rosenberg. The western part of Poland, under German control, was to be annexed to the Reich and Germanized. This meant that the non-German population, more than 8 million, would eventually be expelled from it; for the time being, Germans living until then in the regions now under Soviet influence would be settled there. The central part of German Poland was to accommodate the Polish population, and would be accorded some sort of statehood ('Eine polnische"Staatlichkeit" '). Finally, the eastern sector, situated between the Vistula and the Bug, was to receive the Jews, 'including those from the Reich', as well as other undesirable elements.

(Hitler was no doubt thinking of the gypsies and perhaps of the 'asocials'.)[11]

Hitler probably did not think of this regrouping of nationalities as a definitive solution. He kept in mind his plan of the conquest of Lebensraum to the east, a conquest which would eventually involve the Germanization of territories presently assigned to the Poles and Jews. The latter, in any case, would have to leave Europe sooner or later. It is significant in this regard that, in a speech given on 6 October 1939, Hitler spoke of an 'effort to organize and settle the Jewish problem'.[12] Under the circumstances, with emigration made even more difficult by the war, the resettlement of the Jews on the periphery of the Great Reich would have constituted, in his eyes, a satisfactory interim solution.

This decision flowed logically, it seems to me, from the situation in which he found himself. A European war had broken out, and while he was much more confident than his generals of a victory in the West, he knew that it was not assured yet. At the same time, the situation revived in him the memory of the Great War, reminding him of the resolutions he had made in the 1920s. 'A November 1918 will never again be repeated in the history of Germany!' he proclaimed in his first wartime speech; he would repeat it in public and in private.[13]

Neither revolution nor surrender: and to guard against them he also announced his determination to fight ruthlessly against war profiteers, saboteurs, and defeatists. 'The brave soldier at the front must know that for us his life is more valuable than the lives of traitors to the fatherland,' he proclaimed. 'For the first time in history' it would not be permissible for some to make a profit from the war while others gave their lives.[14] In every respect the concentration of Jews in a clearly defined region must have seemed commendable, if not essential. According to his version of the Great War, their presence closer to home would constitute a danger: danger of revolution in the event of military reversals or internal troubles, and danger to the morale of the population in the event of a prolonged conflict. On 9 May 1940 Goebbels reported in his diary that Hitler flew into a rage upon learning that some Jews had been put to work alongside German crews; Jews were supposed to work only in separate units because they might undermine morale.[15]

The decision to concentrate the Jews on the periphery of the

Reich reveals nothing, however, about Hitler's ultimate intentions. One might maintain, granting him a Machiavellianism of epic proportions, that he chose to assemble the Jews in the outer reaches of the Reich in order to kill them more easily and safely. For that matter, were not most of the extermination camps built in those areas two years later? One can only prove such a scenario by omitting certain important details that lead in an entirely different direction. For at the time Hitler – and this is a generally unrecognized point – was motivated above all by a desire to get rid of the Jews and no longer be burdened with them.

On 17 October 1939, during a period when he was contemplating the creation of a Polish state, he told Keitel, the head of the Wehrmacht's high command (OKW), that the non-annexed part of Poland was to become independent, and that those in charge of this territory would have to permit the Reich to deposit its Jews and Poles there.[16] Three weeks earlier he had said to Dahlerus, a Swedish intermediary, that 'if he reorganized the Polish state, the Jews could find asylum there'.[17] The Polish state in question would have had to be a rump state under Germany's control. By forcing it to accept all the Reich's Jews, Hitler would make a later intervention more difficult for himself, however. Obviously, his main preoccupation was to escape the burden that the concentration of millions of people on a tiny, poor area would entail. He had demonstrated in the past that he had no intention of spending money on the Jews. He was being consistent by seeking to rid himself of a burden that grew heavier in direct ratio to the impoverishment of his victims and to the increase in their numbers.

The emigration of the Jews continued to be promoted, meanwhile, by Heydrich's staff, who made every effort to mitigate the obstacles raised by the war. Even more striking was the expulsion policy carried out along the German-Soviet demarcation line; as we have seen, Heydrich announced on 21 September 1939 that Hitler had approved it. The army had stolen a march on him by ordering, as early as 12 September, the expulsion of the Jews of eastern Upper Silesia into the Russian zone; on 18 September it barred the return of Jews who had fled to the East.[18] But it was the Einsatzgruppen which, in the following months, would proceed with systematic expulsions. While it is difficult to estimate the results, at least several tens of thousands of persons were brutally and under the greatest duress driven to the east, exposed to drowning while crossing the rivers that separated the two countries, exposed also to shooting by their German escorts, and sometimes to being forced back by Soviet sentries. The USSR, which had left her frontier open for several months, finally complained about these crossings; in December 1939 Hans Frank, whom Hitler had named head of the General Government, the non-annexed part of Poland under German control, asked the police to put an end to the actions which were harmful to the 'friendly relations' between the two countries.[19]

Hitler had decided, then, to regroup the Jews in a reservation located at the edge of his empire. But everything continued as if no decision had been made, or at least as if its execution had been lost sight of somewhere along the way. In early October 1939 Eichmann received an order to deport to the General Government a certain number of Jews living in the protectorate of Bohemia-Moravia and in Upper Silesia; the point was to gain experience before moving up to large-scale deportations. Zealous as ever, Eichmann set up an ambitious programme, going so far as to include the Jews of Vienna on his own initiative. Several thousand Jews, volunteers in theory, were brought to Nisko, on the San river near Lublin, to build a receiving and transit camp. The project was scarcely under way when an order from Berlin cancelled the operation. Some of the Jews were driven into the wilderness and left to their own devices; the others spent the winter on the site before receiving authorization to return to their point of departure.

Undertaken under the guise of an improvisation, the 'Nisko action' was in any case destined for major problems. It had been undertaken by exploiting the still embryonic state of the General Government administration. There is no doubt that Frank, once informed, would have raised loud objections, not to mention the army, which had critical need of the railroads. But what doomed it from the start was the arrival in the annexed territories of the first convoys of Germans from the Russian sphere of influence. Here the true emergency lay, and not in the Protectorate or in Austria, since the feeding and lodging of tens of thousands of persons would have to be assured by dispossessing and deporting at least as many non-Germans in the General Government. As a result, Eichmann was called to Berlin to the RSHA where, in December 1939, he was given the directorship of section IV D 4 of the Gestapo, his mission to formulate an overall plan for the evacuations.[20]

In the following months police officials concentrated their efforts on the annexed territories, where two new provinces had been created, the Wartheland and West Prussia. On 30 October 1939 Himmler had made it known that he wanted all Jews – more than 500,000 persons – evacuated from there before February 1940, together with as many Poles as it took to reach a total of a million. The departure of the Jews clearly had priority, but no further mention was made of moving them to the area around Lublin; in the following months they were distributed throughout the whole of General Government. These systematic deportations – since the beginning of the occupation there had been numerous 'unauthorized' deportations – were launched in December 1939. Tens of thousands of Jews and Poles were crammed into freight cars, stripped of everything except a small suitcase, and unloaded several hours, sometimes several days, later, in the General Government, where no provisions had been made for their food or shelter from the rigours of winter; hundreds of people died of the cold.

The zeal of the police was not equal to the job, and it quickly became clear that Himmler had over-extended himself. In the following months, his initial programme would constantly be revised downward before being suspended. The operation had run up against the shortage of transportation, the objections of Goering and of the army, and, finally, Frank's protestations. On 12 February 1940 a high-level meeting under Goering's chairmanship slowed down the enterprise. As usual more preoccupied with economic efficacy than with racial purification, Goering maintained that the evacuations should not impair the smooth functioning of the economy or jeopardize labour in the annexed territories, especially farm workers. Of course it would eventually be incumbent on the General Government to welcome all the Jews of the Great Reich; but that should be effected in an orderly and concerted fashion. This was just what Frank wanted to hear, for he was specifically seeking to make the size of the deportations contingent on the provision of supplies necessary for the maintenance of the new arrivals.

Himmler found himself in a uncomfortable position. He

complained that 'in all likelihood not more than 300,000 persons' had been evacuated thus far. Because of the problems produced by the evacuations and because of the necessities of wartime, he dropped the idea of repatriating several hundred thousand Germans from Lithuania, Bucovina, and Bessarabia. On the other hand, evacuations remained necessary to settle 70,000 Germans from the Baltic states and 130,000 more from Volhynia, evacuations which, he was sure, would be carried out in co-operation with Frank.[21]

Matters only appeared to be settled, however. In the following weeks the SS again quite independently organized several waves of deportations to the General Government; among them, and for the first time, 1,000 Jews from the old Reich in February 1940; their evacuation stirred emotions and protests abroad. As a result of new demands from Frank, Goering announced on 23 March that he was banning all deportations that had not received both his approval and Frank's. Following discussions with Frank, Himmler agreed to suspend all further deportations of Jews until August.

After six months of effort, Himmler could gauge the failure of his ambitions. It had first been a matter of expelling all non-Germans from the annexed territories; then at least all the Jews, a goal now deferred until summer. As for deporting the Jews from the old Reich, while the intention had been affirmed by Goering on 12 February, nothing seemed to have been done to implement it. In fact, priority had been given to settling the Germans from abroad; this was the only argument at Himmler's disposal to make Frank accept the convoys of freezing, starving people he was sending him.

During this time, the idea of a Jewish reservation had moved further and further into the background. Had it only been a delusion? In addition to the practical problems we have just considered, uncertainty about the reality of the goal never seems to have been dispelled. Even the RSHA was not very clear about it at the end of December 1939. Invited to give its opinion prior to meeting of the department heads with Heydrich, the anti-Jewish branch put out a memorandum titled 'Final Solution of the Jewish Problem in Germany': this was one of the first instances of that formula which would be used with increasing frequency before undergoing, in 1941, a decisive change of meaning. The author of this document wondered what would become of the Jews: would they wind up as charges of a future Polish state, or would they live in reservation in one of Germany's dependent territories? In the latter case, the author pronounced himself in favour of self-administration under German control; and, still in that case, supposed it would have to be decided whether or not emigration should continue. From the foreign-policy point of view, finally, he opined, 'reservation would be a good means of exerting pressure on the western powers. Perhaps by this method we could, at the conclusion of the peace treaty, raise the question of a global solution' – a solution which would obviously have to take the form of a world reservation for Jews.[22]

It does not appear that the matter was clarified during the following weeks. During the 12 February meeting Himmler mentioned that the region around Lublin would be transformed into a Jewish reservation. But he spoke of it in a manner that indicated it was not on the agenda. Because of this projected reservation, he declared, it would 'in all likelihood be necessary' to transfer the some 30,000 Germans living around Lublin back to the Reich. The idea of reservation persisted, then, but remained nebulous. Frank heard about it and was extremely displeased,[23] but nothing indicates that he received any instructions from Hitler as to its implementation. In April 1940 the official in charge of Jewish questions in his administration was still no further forward than calling for a preliminary investigation of zones that might lend themselves to the establishment of a Jewish reservation.[24]

The reason for this state of uncertainty must be sought in the attitude of Hitler himself, who seemed quickly to lose interest in the project. On 12 March 1940 he declared that the Jewish question was one of space, and that he had none at his disposal. The establishment of a Jewish state around Lublin, he added, would not be a solution, for the Jews would be too crowded together to achieve an acceptable standard of living.[25] He was speaking to Colin Ross, a Nazi propagandist who was asking him to formulate, for the American public, the solution he visualized for the 'Jewish problem'. The reason Hitler gave to explain his abandonment of the projected reservation had promotional value, then; it does not seem any less significant.

It confirms, in fact, that he was well aware of the misery the creation of a Jewish reservation would force the Jews to live in. He was not concerned about their standard of living, but he thought he was obliged to care, because of international opinion, above all, in this case, American opinion – a significant point, since the decision for extermination would mean a complete end to all considerations of this kind. His attitude also confirms, *a contrario*, that if he was seduced in September and October of 1939 by the idea of deporting the Jews to the region around Lublin, it was because he hoped to place them in the custody of the Polish rump state he planned to create at the time. It is not surprising that he lost all interest in the project when, at the end of October, the existence of such a state ceased to be on the agenda. Finally, since he had never visualized this solution as anything but temporary, its abandonment must have been all the easier. Preparations for the western campaign obsessed him: everything depended on its outcome.

By the spring of 1940, Hitler's point of view must have been known to his entourage. During May, probably after the first successes of the French campaign, Himmler wrote a memorandum on the fate of non-Germans in Poland in which he proposed methods for divesting them of their national conscience and rendering them docile to the Nazi yoke. As for the 'Jewish problem', he hoped to make it disappear completely through the emigration of all Jews to Africa or to a colony elsewhere. The conception and tone of the memorandum indicate that Himmler must have been given a global mandate, that Hitler had turned to him to settle the 'Jewish question'. That the solution must be something other than extermination is clear enough from his proposals. Another passage from the text confirms this.

After recommending that Polish children with German blood be separated from their parents and sent to school in the Reich, he wrote, 'Tragic and barbaric as it may be for each individual case, this method is nevertheless the most compassionate and the best if, through personal conviction, we reject as contrary to the German spirit [*ungermanisch*] and as impossible the Bolshevik method of the physical extermination of a people . . .' On 28 May he submitted this memorandum to Hitler, who found it 'very good and right' and agreed that it be shown to Frank and to the Gauleiters of the annexed territories for use as a guideline.[26]

A reservation in Poland was no longer on the cards. Before long, a new project consistent with the ideas expressed by

Himmler won the minds of the Nazi leaders: the deportation of the Jews to the French colony of Madagascar. Probably because of its distance and insular character, Madagascar had for several years fired the imagination of European anti-Semites. In 1938, as we have seen, various Nazi leaders, including Hitler, made reference to it. The defeat of France and the presumably imminent conclusion of a peace treaty with Great Britain suddenly brought the idea into the realm of the possible.

In the first days of June, the specialist on Jewish questions at the Ministry of Foreign Affairs put out a memorandum in which he proposed concentrating the Jews in Madagascar. The RSHA greeted it with enthusiasm and set about drawing up a detailed plan. Anxious not to lose ground, Heydrich wrote to von Ribbentrop on 24 June reminding him that he (Heydrich) had been charged with handling the Jewish question through emigration. Since the obstacles encountered now forced him to seek a territorial solution, he wanted to be associated with the project under consideration.[27] This news rapidly spread through high Nazi circles and leaked abroad.[28]

Hitler also endorsed the plan. On 20 June he held a meeting with the head of the German navy, Admiral Raeder, in Keitel's presence. Raeder noted that 'the Führer wanted to use Madagascar to harbour the Jews under the aegis of the French'.[29] While the RSHA was working out a plan based on the idea that the reservation would be placed under German control, and more precisely under the control of the SS, Hitler saw things differently, in a way that was perfectly consistent with the position he had taken in October 1939 about the Lublin reservation. Now, as then, he expressed his desire to be rid of the Jews altogether and to be relieved of the responsibility for their fate.

On 8 July he returned to the subject in a conversation with Frank. A few days later, the latter announced with satisfaction to his associates in Cracow that the deportations of Jews to the General Government would definitively cease. It was planned to deport all the Jews, as soon as possible after the signing of the peace treaty, to an African or American colony, probably Madagascar.[30] As a result, he halted all building of ghettos, then under construction. In mid-August Goebbels wrote in his journal, reporting on the content of a conversation with Hitler, that the Jews would be shipped to Madagascar where they could have their own state.[31]

After the spectacular defeat of France, Hitler was at the zenith of his power and prestige. In the midst of this euphoric atmosphere, he buoyantly seized on a plan that seemed to offer a solution to the 'Jewish question'. Since 1938, as we have seen, he had expressed his desire to have that question settled for all of Europe. In the summer of 1940, he was in a position to fulfil that desire, if not entirely, at least to a large extent by making the necessary arrangements in the conquered countries and by rallying his allies and satellites. To Otto Abetz, who was on his way to Paris to advise the German military commanders on relations with the Vichy government, he declared in early August that he was committed to making all the Jews leave Europe after the war.[32] The new ambassador was therefore clear about what policy to pursue. As for the allies and satellites, they soon saw which way the wind was blowing. As a Hungarian diplomat wrote to his Minister on 10 September, radical steps regarding the 'Jewish problem' would be necessary if Hungary wished to develop close ties with Berlin and Rome.[33]

But the deportation of Jews overseas would require peacetime conditions: Germany did not have supremacy at sea. Without the consent or forbearance of Great Britain, the Madagascar project had no future. Hitler hoped that the fall of France would bring London to the bargaining table to conclude a compromise peace. But the British leaders refused to yield, despite their critical situation, and indicated their determination to continue the war. Thus defied, Hitler prepared for the invasion of the British isles, only too aware that his adversary's maritime superiority made the outcome uncertain, if not risky; in September he postponed the operation until the following spring. His attempts to break the enemy with his air power had failed during the first weeks of autumn, and he realized that the conflict would not soon be over.

The realization of the Madagascar project was now deferred to an ill-defined future. Yet Hitler does not seem to have abandoned the idea willingly. To Rosenberg, who wanted to know if he could publish an article titled 'The Jews in Madagascar', Bormann replied on 3 November that, after learning of the article, the Führer had decided that it should not appear for the moment, but 'perhaps in a few months'.[34] At the end of the month, during a conversation with a Hungarian diplomat, Hitler said that he saw in the settlement of the Jewish question in Europe one of the greatest tasks of the postwar period and that he intended, during the peace negotiations, to force France to place one of her possessions at his disposition.[35] Madagascar was just one destination among others; Hitler would refer to it again during the following months. There seems no possible doubt about his wish to send the Jews overseas or about his hope to do so in the near future.

Like the Lublin plan, the Madagascar project was proving to be impracticable. Both had been adopted by Hitler during uncertain times which had soon invalidated them. The first, in any event, would only have been a temporary measure. The second, on the other hand, purported to offer a definitive solution. Ephemeral as they were, these projects were seriously considered, the second in particular.[36] They both portray a Hitler eager to shift the burden of supporting this mass of deportees onto some other country. If the plan had ever been effected, the concentration of millions of people in a reservation would, without question, have claimed untold numbers of victims. Hitler knew this very well, and did not care; others would have to take responsibility for the fate of the deportees.

The years of success, at any rate, did not bring Hitler to decide on extermination. The departure of the European Jews, and their confinement in a distant territory, would suffice to solve the problem. His anti-Jewish policy continued to depend directly on his strategic situation which, to a certain extent, also coloured his perception of the enemy. An examination of his attitudes toward the Jews from 1939 to 1941 shows that they mirrored the ups and downs of his strategic position between the signing of the alliance with the USSR and his decision to revoke it.

One can see to what extent anti-Semitism was central to his world vision by considering the interpretation he gave to the German-Soviet pact. In his eyes, the Bolshevik regime was a Jewish regime par excellence. And yet this regime, which should have been his mortal enemy, had agreed to reach an accord with him. This was because, as he explained to Mussolini on 18 March 1940, the Georgian Stalin had succeeded in gaining the upper hand and suppressing Jewish influence; the Soviet Union was now reunited with eternal Muscovy.[37] Hitler was anything but a cynic: he preferred to distort reality rather than let it interfere with his system of analysing the world. But the essential, here, is that the German-Soviet pact must, in his eyes, have signalled the dwindling of Jewish power and an increased likelihood of his own success.

During the 'phony war' of 1939–40, Hitler viewed the future with confidence. In his notebooks, Goebbels portrays him redrawing the map of Europe, restoring to Germany the base she had before the Peace of Westphalia, designating Burgundy as a territory for colonization by the Germans of South Tyrol, evoking the future domination of the world.[38] A feeling of confidence was also evident in the references to the Jews and their role in his speeches. While he always denounced them with vehemence, he did not charge them with the sole responsibility for the war. The instigators of the war were 'Jews and non-Jews'; other forces (plutocrats, reactionaries, democrats, capitalists, etc.) shared the blame on an equal basis with them.[39] He had beaten them in Germany, and he would do the same in the battle he was currently waging abroad.[40] He even used an unaccustomed tone of irony on occasion: thus he denounced the 'dialect' of the propagandists of Radio London.[41]

Even more strikingly, he spoke of the Jews as 'stupid' adversaries, who had proved not to be as powerful as he himself had always claimed and believed. On 24 February 1940 he ranked them among the races victimized by British manipulation: they too had been exploited by Great Britain, since the Balfour Declaration had promised them a land already awarded to the Arabs.[42] On 25 April 1940, Goebbels noted, Hitler had said that, 'all things considered, the Jews are still very stupid'.[43] On 8 November 1940, the Führer declared before the party old guard in Munich that he had always been of the opinion that there was 'no people more stupid than the Jewish people'. A few minutes earlier, however, he had endowed them with 'satanic power', a power that had long dominated Germany and declared war on the young Nazi movement before succumbing to its victorious blows.[44] In short, during this period, he had much more contempt than fear for the Jews, even though the latter sentiment had certainly not disappeared: for that matter, can a satanic power be entirely stupid?

All this makes it highly unlikely that Hitler harboured a scheme for unconditional extermination. A passage from Goebbels's notebooks is interesting in this regard. On 5 December 1939, the day after a talk with Hitler during which the Jews had been discussed at length, Goebbels wrote that the Führer shared his point of view: 'We must exorcise the Jewish danger. But it will emerge again in a few generations. There is no antidote for it.'[45] These remarks are characteristic of Nazi hubris, of the feverish preoccupation of the masters of the Reich with the future of the German nation, with their ambition to create a deathless work. It is all the more striking that the idea of extermination did not surface here, when it could have served as the 'antidote' for the anxiety voiced. Hitler was not loath to discuss exterminatory solutions among his peers; but the projected victims were not the Jews. Goebbels noted, on 17 August 1940, that in the same conversation during which Hitler had talked about shipping the Jews to Madagascar, he had made violent statements against criminals, and especially against 'asocial elements', which must be exterminated rather than left alive to foment a future revolution.[46]

By the summer of 1940, Hitler was confronted with a new strategic situation: his great successes were bringing with them great dangers. British resistance raised the spectre of a war that would last indefinitely, neither antagonist having the means to destroy the other. But while the Reich had already enlisted most of her available support, Britain could still hope for the rallying of the neutral powers, the formidable reinforcement of the United States and, perhaps, some day of the USSR. In the summer of 1939, Hitler had been able to leave the United States out of his strategic calculations; the weakness of her armaments, like the strength of her isolationism, made intervention on her part most improbable. A year later, the American factor loomed at the heart of his anxious scheming.

The United States had made it abundantly clear that she would not accept the defeat of Britain and desired instead the demise of Nazi Germany; she was supplying London with increasing aid and was arming herself at full tilt. In September 1940, by delivering some fifty destroyers in return for the leasing of certain bases in the western hemisphere, she overstepped her neutral status and came close to belligerence. Although Hitler knew that US intervention was not to be feared in the near future and that it would take time – one or two years – for American military capability to carry any weight, he also knew that the USA would then decisively tip the balance of power. Time was against him; to put off the fateful day as long as possible, he conducted a policy of extreme prudence toward the USA, doing his utmost to avoid anything that might encourage or precipitate her entry into the war. For this reason he steadfastly resisted the pressure exerted by Admiral Raeder, partisan of an aggressive naval policy toward a nation he considered a *de facto* belligerent power.

To all this was added the Soviet factor, less feared but much harder to bear. Hitler saw Stalin take advantage of the situation, swallowing up the Baltic countries during the defeat of France, coercing Romania to cede Bessarabia and part of Bucovinia, and not troubling to conceal his appetite for other portions of the Balkans. Of course he knew that Moscow was not in a position to break their pact, and that Stalin was not considering it. More than the fear of an improbable and distant Russian entry into the war, it was a strategic argument, combined with his lifelong dreams of expansion, that made him visualize turning against his ally. In his opinion, Great Britain persevered in the war because she hoped that the USA and the USSR would some day rally to her cause. If the latter were crushed by another blitzkrieg, London would have no choice but to conclude a peace – and all the more so since the probability of an American intervention would also be reduced. Hitler assumed, in effect, that the defeat of the Soviet Union would relieve Japan of all pressure on her western flank and make her a formidable foe for the United States. At worst, the conquest of Russia would place the Reich in the best position for continuing the war against the Anglo-Saxons.

Hitler formulated this strategy at the end of July 1940. A campaign against the USSR could not be launched until the following spring, and the final decision was only made in December. In the meantime he applied himself to the implementation of an interim strategy aimed at neutralizing the United States and isolating Great Britain. In September the Reich signed a tripartite pact with Italy and Japan to dissuade the United States from abandoning her role as spectator. Concurrently, he bent his efforts to ousting Great Britain from the Mediterranean, which required, besides the co-operation of an Italy jealous of any encroachment on her sphere of influence, the consent of Spain and, if possible, of Vichy France. Furthermore, to isolate the enemy completely, a diplomatic campaign was launched with the aim of creating an anti-British bloc which Russia herself was invited to join. Hitler does not seem to have expected much from this campaign, conceived and animated by von Ribbentrop. A rift between London and Moscow would have constituted a short-term success, without hindering military plans for the following spring. The talks he held with Molotov in Berlin in early November confirmed that Stalin meant to exploit his position without breaking with London; this strengthened his intention of crushing the last remaining Continental power.

By the end of 1940 it was clear that Hitler's interim strategy had not borne the anticipated fruit. Franco's prudent neutrality made it impossible to take Gibraltar and eliminate the British presence from the Mediterranean. At the same time, Mussolini's rout in Greece made a German intervention in the Balkans necessary the following spring, if only to secure the region for the duration of the Eastern campaign. The United States, far from having been intimidated by the tripartite pact, had hardened its attitude toward the involved powers, henceforth seen as so many members of a global conspiracy. And the re-election of Roosevelt, who made no secret of his hostility to Nazi Germany, boded ill for the future.

More than ever, Hitler had to rely on the smooth running of the campaign against the Soviet Union (codenamed Barbarossa). No doubt he also seized the opportunity to regain the path to his fundamental goal, the conquest of *Lebensraum*. Both strategic measure and ideological mission, the war against the Soviet Union represented a doubly important gamble, a gamble he was committed to winning, but of whose high stakes he was only too aware. As he said to his military leaders on 9 January 1941, if Germany one day should have to face the combined forces of Great Britain, the USA, and the USSR, she would find herself 'in a very difficult situation'.[47]

In January 1941, he told Mussolini that as long as Stalin was alive, Germany had nothing to fear, but that the day he died the Jews would take centre stage again.[48] The Jewish peril represented by the Soviet regime had only been in eclipse; now it rose up again before him in all its magnitude. But the clearest sign of resurgence of Hitler's idea of the 'satanic power' of the Jews can be found in his public reiteration of his prophecy of January 1939.

At that time, from the rostrum of the Reichstag, he had vowed to exterminate the Jews if another world war should break out. The subject did not appear again in his speeches, and I could find no trace of it in what has come down to us of his private remarks. Two years later, on 30 January 1941, shortly after confirming his decision to invade Russia, he publicly repeated his prophecy, thereby revealing that it had always lurked in some recess of his mind and that, on the eve of major events, he once again needed to impart his deepest purpose to the world. In this speech he referred to his remarks of January 1939, but ascribing them to 1 September 1939. If this error has a significance, it means that he saw in the invasion of Poland the point of departure for the situation in which he now found himself, a situation whose dangers he could almost smell. Once again, he referred to the United States. But now he explicitly alluded to possible US intervention in Europe, and announced his determination to fight. As for the prophecy itself, he formulated it in a slightly different way, not using (as in 1939) the word 'annihilation', but indicating in vaguer terms that the role of the Jews in Europe would be terminated. However, he left unchanged the connection he had made between his avowed retribution and the escalation of the war to include the whole world: 'if the rest of the world is effectively thrust by the Jews into a general war, that will be the end of Jewry's role in Europe!'[49]

Had Hitler changed his mind and decided to exterminate the European Jews? If he was serious in making these statements, as I believe he was, if he wanted to get a message across, then such a decision was improbable at that date. Once again, he had qualified his statement as prophecy. He meant, as in 1939, to announce a future event whose occurrence he linked to one condition: the development of a 'world war' or a 'general war', a situation whose probability had greatly increased since January 1939 but which had not come to pass by the beginning of 1941 and which he himself did not deem imminent. At the time he repeated his prophecy, he was clear about the British determination to resist, which he attributed to Jewish influence. He saw the Jewish peril rise again in the Soviet Union, which he had decided to crush with a blitzkrieg. Finally, looming on his horizon was the hostility of the United States, where Jewish influence was growing dangerously but had not yet won the day. A prolongation and a spreading of the conflict had certainly become serious threats; perhaps he was starting to feel haunted by the prospect of another four-year war. But only the course of events in the months following the launching of Operation Barbarossa would enable him to decide.

Sources which could enlighten us about his thoughts between the autumn of 1940 and June 1941 are few and far between, but without exception they indicate that he still espoused the idea of deporting the European Jews and settling them somewhere. According to notes kept by Major Engel, a representative of the army (notes reconstructed after the fact and unreliably dated, but whose contents give every appearance of authenticity), Hitler spoke at length about the Jewish question during a conversation which Engel places on 2 February 1941, and which took place in the presence of Keitel, Bormann, Ley, and Speer. Hitler declared that, while the war offered an opportunity to settle the Jewish question more rapidly, notably by placing a number of countries under the Reich influence, it also raised new difficulties. The problem was where he 'could put these several million Jews'. He intended to ask France to place Madagascar at his disposal. To Bormann, who had asked how the Jews could be transported there in wartime, he answered that he would have to think about it, but that he had no desire to lose any ships. He concluded by saying that he 'now saw certain things in a different light, which was not really more favourable'.[50] Obviously, he was not clear about the exact solution to the problem he had set himself; but he remained attached to the idea of a territorial solution. His final phrase might indicate a hardening of attitude, but hardly an extermination plan.

Goebbels noted after talks with Hitler on two occasions during this period, in November 1940 and March 1941, that one day the Jews would be deported from Europe; no territory of destination was mentioned.[51] In April 1941, after mentioning to a Hungarian diplomat the expulsion of the Poles from the Wartheland, Hitler went on about the

'Jewish question', declaring that it must be solved on a European level by the resettlement of the Jews. Millions of Europeans had had to relocate abroad in the past; he did not see the slightest inhumanity in now forcing the Jews to emigrate, and as second-class travellers.[52] On 2 June 1941, scarcely three weeks before the start of the Russian campaign, he said to Mussolini that all Jews must leave Europe after the war and that 'perhaps' they could be settled in Madagascar.[53]

One cannot, of course, rule out the possibility that he systematically concealed his deepest purpose. But then one must also admit that he conducted, or allowed the machinery of his regime to conduct, a policy which did not correspond to his secret wishes. During this period, in fact, there is no apparent break with the course followed in the preceding years. As before, a cordon-sanitaire policy was designed to forestall the return or the increase in number of Jews in the German sphere of influence. In August 1940, Hitler himself directed Abetz not to let Jews who had fled the German advance return to occupied France.[54] And in April 1941 he intervened to prohibit Polish Jews from being brought into the Reich to supplement the manpower shortage, even though all the necessary arrangements, including Goering's approval, had already been made.[55]

Whenever the opportunity presented itself, it was the policy of expulsion that was put into practice. In July 1940 the Gauleiters Wagner and Bürckel, who had been given the task of Germanizing Alsace and Lorraine, began shipping waves of nearly a quarter of a million French citizens, among them the Jews of the region, to Vichy France. In October they did the same, with Hitler's consent, to at least 6,500 German Jews living in their *Gaue*, the Bade and the Palatinate; the moment, no doubt, seemed propitious for rendering these districts 'judenfrei'.[56]

The deportation policy in the General Government, from the incorporated territories, also remained in effect, even intensifying at the end of 1940. To Frank's great displeasure, Hitler persisted in designating the General Government as the reception centre for Poles living in the Reich's new territories. According to what Frank later reported, Hitler explained to him on 4 November 1940 that the expulsion of the Poles must be accomplished immediately since, after the war, it might arouse international protest – a reason which reveals preoccupations quite difficult to reconcile with ideas of extermination.[57]

At the beginning of 1941 the RSHA worked out an evacuation plan that involved 831,000 persons, Jews and Poles, living in the annexed territories. Once again Himmler's vision was grandiose, too grandiose, and his evacuation plan met the same fate as his earlier efforts. In mid-March 1941, in the face of mounting protestations from the army, which needed the railway system for its preparations for the Russian campaign, his plan was cancelled before it even got off the ground. It was no longer a question of deporting all the Jews from the Great Reich to the General Government, even as a temporary measure. In December 1940, it is true, Hitler authorized the deportation of 60,000 Jews living in Vienna. But that action, which barely got under way and was prompted by the housing crisis in Vienna, was presented as an emergency measure which waived the currently accepted rule that the departure of the Jews would take place after the war.[58]

The emigration policy, then, continued to be adamantly pursued. Since the war made this increasingly difficult, it became necessary to set priorities. It is clear from a memorandum from the RSHA dated 20 May 1941 that Goering wished the emigration of German Jews to be expedited despite the wartime conditions. As a result, the RSHA decided emigration would be denied to the Jews of Belgium and occupied France: the meagre quotas allotted by foreign countries were to be saved for German Jews.[59]

As these policies were carried out, preparations for the postwar solution were being stepped up. Since the summer of 1940, sectors of the bureaucracy directly involved had been busying themselves laying the necessary foundations for the deportation of the Jews from Europe. The Ministry of the Interior undertook to write a law designed to divest German Jews of their nationality; after many drafts and counter-drafts, it would be enacted at the end of 1941, in an entirely different context. And while Eichmann, in Berlin, polished the Madagascar plan with the help of representatives from over fifteen other departments,[60] anti-Jewish advisers were being dispatched to occupied or friendly countries to prepare for the coming great evacuation. The mission of these advisers was to introduce to all of Nazi Europe the anti-Semitic programme operating in Germany.

Through the registration of Jews, their dispossession, their exclusion from society, and, if possible, their concentration, the programme sought to create the conditions necessary for a later deportation. The work of these advisers would prove useful later, during the extermination; but this had not been its original task.

The Nazi police apparatus spoke of this coming deportation as the 'final solution', an expression that appeared, as we have seen, at the end of 1939 and had gained much wider use by the summer of 1940, notably in a formula that soon became stereotyped: 'in consideration of the approach of the final solution to the Jewish question'. This portentous formula confused many historians, as it would later be used to designate extermination. Because it contained this formula, the RSHA memorandum of 20 May 1941, mentioned above, regularly came to be cited as proof of the existence of an extermination plan. The sentence in which it is inserted, however, shows that the hour of genocide had not yet come: 'In consideration of the approach of the final solution to the Jewish question, the immigration of Jews into territories occupied by us must be prevented.'[61] This prescription made no sense unless the goal of this final solution was to empty the Nazi sphere of its Jews, and not to amass as many as possible in it in order to exterminate them.

Along with Hitler, the police chiefs soon realized that the Madagascar plan was impracticable. They nevertheless continued to work in the same direction, simply leaving the matter of the territory of destination open. On 5 February 1941 Heydrich defined the 'final solution' as the transfer of the Jews to a country to be determined later. In Paris, the head of the Sipo-SD had expressed it similarly a few weeks earlier when, speaking of the 'plan for the final solution', he referred to the evacuation of the Jews 'to a territory yet to be determined'.[62] The Jews would leave Europe after the end of the war: that was all the Nazi police needed to know in order to accomplish their task.

Nothing in all this indicates that any new developments occurred. Preparations with a view to an extermination operation on a European scale were not in evidence during this period; we shall see that they did not appear until a later date. As for Hitler's opinions and interventions, they give no indication whatsoever of any intentions along those lines. We cannot ignore the hypothesis of his duplicity, but the available documentation leads us to conclude that he entertained a double train of thought about the Jews: on the one hand, a course of vengeance in the event of failure; on the other, because he believed or wanted to believe in his success, the intention of settling the 'Jewish problem' through a territorial initiative, in Madagascar or elsewhere, a solution which would be effected soon after the war.[63]

We shall only subscribe provisionally to this conclusion; in the next chapter we shall investigate whether or not a policy of extermination was conceived and readied for the Soviet Jews. I raise first a point that is not without importance, the attitude of Hitler's lieutenants. To what extent were they in agreement with the ideas of their leader? A difficult question, to which I have no sure answer. It seems to me that they did not share Hitler's major obsessions, and that he was alone in considering the hypothesis of exterminating the Jews. In 1940 the future perpetrators of the genocide were not thinking along those lines. We need only recall the memorandum put out by Himmler in May 1940, in which he rejected the physical extermination of a people as both 'impossible' and 'contrary to the German nature'. Two months later, in a note of 2 July 1940 addressed to his superior, Heydrich brought up the friction with the army caused by the liquidation 'by the thousands' of the Polish elite, and described these measures as 'extraordinarily radical'.[64] Clearly he had no conception of the task that would fall on his shoulders a short time later. Not to mention Goering, whose anti-Semitism was robust, but always sensitive to practical considerations.

It would be interesting to know how these men perceived the extermination-minded statements of their leader. The day after Hitler's speech of 30 January 1939, Goebbels summarized its main points in his diary, but did not mention the prophecy.[65] The only reference he made to it before the start of the Russian campaign is dated 20 June 1941. The evening before he had visited Hitler with Frank, who spoke about the situation in the General Government and probably described the miserable lives of the Jews there. Goebbels wrote: 'Jewry is slowly dying out in Poland. A just punishment for their provocative intrigues and hostile manipulations. The Führer rightly prophesied it to the Jews.'[66] We can see that he had not understood his leader's prophecy correctly, and had interpreted it in a relatively non-radical way. We can also see that, if he did not yet envision extermination, he nevertheless accepted the idea of decimation.

Several echelons below Goebbels, Adolf Eichmann does not seem to have taken the Führer's words literally either. Before his judges in Jerusalem, he stated that he had known about Hitler's prophecy but had seen it as a piece of propaganda.[67] It is hardly likely that it escaped the attention of men like Himmler and Heydrich. While nothing indicates that they were inspired to launch initiatives or make proposals, they at least must have realized that a more radical prospect existed, and glimpsed what they themselves may not have imagined.

More generally, it is important to recognize the development of a climate that would permit, once the prophecy had become an order, the execution of this order. Among Nazi leaders who had to cope with it in one way or another, the 'Jewish question' was starting to cause serious frustrations. Hitler tirelessly emphasized his determination to free Germany and Europe of Jews. It became a quasi-religious mission, or at least an affair of state that none of his lieutenants could afford not to be involved in, at the risk of losing influence. But the 'final solution' constantly receded as they advanced toward it, while the number of Jews subject to their rule swelled with each conquest.

The Gauleiters whose territories contained many Jews were the most exposed to the pressures of Hitler's anti-Semitic fanaticism. Thus Goebbels, among other things the Gauleiter of Berlin, was irritated to the point of obsession by the number of Jews living there. To get them out was his ambition, in which the demands of his own anti-Semitism were fused with the dictates of his lust for power. His diaries show that he continually raised the subject during conversations with Hitler. Lacking a means actually to expel them, he made myriad proposals for widening their separation from the German people. The pressure therefore worked both ways; the zeal of his lieutenants hammered home to Hitler the increasingly burdensome absence of a solution to the 'Jewish problem'.

In the eastern territories the situation was no less aggravating to those in charge, whether to Frank or to Greiser, the Gauleiter of the Wartheland, where the majority of Jews still in the annexed territories lived. While Greiser made every effort to send his Jews to the General Government, Frank stubbornly resisted, waiting impatiently for the day when his territory also would be rid of them. Both were driven to take steps they believed would be temporary. The imposition of forced labour, the wearing of a distinguishing badge, and the creation of Jewish councils to serve as intermediaries with the occupying forces – all this was put in place soon after the arrival of German troops. In the Wartheland, the Jews were fairly rapidly regrouped in ghettos cut off from the rest of the city, the largest being the ghetto in Lodz (Litzmannstadt), which was closed on 1 May 1940. In the General Government the movement was belated and unsystematic. The Warsaw ghetto was established in November 1940, modelled on the one in Lodz; those in Cracow and Lublin in March 1941; while a good number of cities had no ghettos until the end of 1941, or even 1942.

At first, closed ghettos like the ones in Lodz and Warsaw served as extortion centres for their unfortunate inhabitants: all their money and what remained of their belongings had to go for food necessary for their survival. When famine and epidemics set in, creating an appalling death rate, the Nazi administration was forced to take a stand. Some ghetto officials were prepared to let the famine take its toll; they anticipated the decimation, if not the obliteration, of the Jewish population. But their view was not accepted, and another policy prevailed: work would be provided for the ghetto Jews in return for food.[68]

After aggravating conditions with measures like confinement in ghettos, and then allowing things to deteriorate completely, Nazi leaders in the east finally ended by 'normalizing' the situation. The presence of the Jews was only temporary, they reasoned; there was no point in worrying unduly about their fate. Furthermore, the deterioration of their living conditions provided an opportune argument with which to impress on Berlin the urgency of some sort of solution. But when it became clear that the consequence of this attitude would be the death by starvation of hundreds of thousands of persons, a decision was made which involved organizing the survival of the Jewish population for an indefinite period. Nazi leaders none the less continued to voice their wish to be rid of the Jews as soon as possible. But it seems that a change of heart had occurred, a change they could not express, but one whose effects we shall see later. Jews who worked had their advantages: the exploitation of their labour proved profitable. But Jews incapable of work were dead weights, whose disappearance no one would regret.

Himmler also must have felt that things were dragging out. The deportation of the Jews from Europe was receding into the distance: could other means not be found? He knew about 'Operation Euthanasia' and the methods employed; the technical services of the criminal police had contributed to their refinement. In early 1941 he asked Bouhler, the head of the Führer's chancellery, for his organization's help in killing the disabled and incurable prisoners in his concentration camps. The operation, carried out under the code name '14 f 13', would claim about 20,000 victims. Gassing was an efficient method which could easily be extended to other categories of people. But Himmler did not yet contemplate extending it to the Jews.

In the Nuremberg trials Victor Brack, one of the top men in the Führer's chancellery and the guiding spirit of 'Operation Euthanasia,' reported that Himmler had spoken to him in January 1941 about his wish to sterilize the Jews, and had asked him to research the possibilities of effecting a mass sterilization.[69] On 28 March 1941 Brack reported the results of his investigation: the thing was feasible, and he would be available for whatever 'theoretical or practical' developments might come next. Himmler answered six weeks later that he had read his report with interest and looked forward to discussing it with him at the earliest opportunity.[70] The matter rested there; it was not until 1942 that Himmler again showed interest in the sterilization of entire populations. In the meantime the extermination of the Jews had begun, an extermination which, early in 1941, Himmler did not see as the solution to his problem.

But so many things were unforeseeable, early in 1941. In the little town of Auschwitz, in German-annexed Poland, a concentration camp for Polish political prisoners had been built in 1940. At the beginning of the following year it was decided to enlarge it, and to add on a camp intended to hold 100,000 future Soviet prisoners-of-war. The 6,000 Jews living in Auschwitz were evicted from their lodgings in March 1941, and settled in neighbouring towns.[71] There the Nazis would later hunt them down, returning them to their point of departure, which had been transformed meanwhile into an extermination site.

4

The Fate of the Soviet Jews

On 22 June 1941 the German army stormed across the Soviet frontier, overwhelming a poorly prepared enemy. As it penetrated deeper into the immense country, units of the police and the SS operated behind the front lines, waging an unprecedented campaign of murder against the Jewish population. Before long, mass shootings of an incredible barbarity were taking place. Here, among many other accounts, is the testimony given at Nuremberg by a German civilian living in Russia who, hearing the sound of gunfire, became the shocked spectator of one of these executions:

> I went around the mound of earth and found myself in front of a gigantic trench. The people in it were so tightly wedged together that all one could see was their heads. Some of the wounded were still moving. A few raised an arm or turned their heads to show that they were still alive. The trench was already three-quarters full. In my estimation, it contained about a thousand people. I looked around for the executioner. He was an SS officer who was sitting on the edge of the trench, his legs dangling into the hole, a submachine-gun across his knees, smoking a cigarette. The victims, stark naked, came down a flight of steps dug into the dirt wall and stumbled across the heads of the dead and dying until they reached the place the SS officer indicated. Then they lay down on top of the people who had already been executed. A few caressed the survivors and spoke to them in hushed voices. Next I heard a series of shots.[1]

About 500,000 Jews – men, women, and children – were killed in this fashion in 1941 alone; at least as many would meet the same fate in the following years. The war against the USSR thus marked an extraordinary radicalization of anti-Semitic action: the murderous potential of Nazism had emerged in all its magnitude. In view of these massacres, and of the measures that would soon be taken to kill the European Jews, it is natural to think that the decision for extermination was made before 22 June 1941. Most historians have seen it that way: the death sentence must have been pronounced during preparations for the Russian campaign, at the latest in the spring of 1941.[2]

This interpretation of events has worked its way into history books. It is supported, however, only by limited and flimsy source material, and by a debatable vision of Hitlerian ideology. Hitler always associated Bolshevism with Judaism: having decided to destroy the one, he had to do the same to the other. Or again: the acquisition of an empire to the east was indissolubly linked in his mind to the destruction of the Jews. Whatever truth they may have, these deductive arguments run up against a problem of chronology. The facts at our disposal indicate that preparations for killing the European Jews did not begin before early autumn. If the decision had been made in the spring, how to explain such a delay in its execution?

The problem can be circumvented by claiming that there were two extermination orders: one in the spring, concerning Russian Jews, the other in the summer, for the rest of the European Jews.[3] The motives for this dual decision still require a convincing explanation. But the fundamental obstacle lies elsewhere: there are good reasons for questioning the existence of the first of these decisions. Undeniably, extermination of the Soviet Jews began during the Russian campaign. But while the campaign of extermination has been proved to have been operative in September 1941, can the same be said for the preceding summer? The space of two or three months may not be much of a time gap, but there are situations in which a few weeks can rock the world.[4]

Here the historian enters a realm of deepening shadows. There is nothing to enlighten him about the conversations that took place between Hitler and Himmler, the proposals made, the initiatives taken, or the orders given. To compensate for the paucity of documentation, his only solution is to focus his research at the level of those involved, great and small, and to try to reconstruct the goals set and the policy implemented during the first months of the Russian campaign: a campaign which, in the minds of Nazi leaders, would only last the summer.

Military and political preparations were begun early in the

year. In March Hitler informed his generals of his goals and the manner in which he wished to see them achieved. The coming campaign, he told them, was not to be an ordinary war, but a fight to the death between two ideologies: he was not going to war to spare the enemy, but to annihilate him. The Soviet state must be destroyed through the use of 'the most brutal violence'. His aim was the elimination of communist officials and of the 'Judeo-Bolshevik intelligentsia'.

As for the future, he anticipated the formation of several satellite states in which, under no circumstances, would a new ruling class be allowed to emerge. He expected the army to understand that the war in the east would be very different from the one waged in western Europe: communist officials were all criminals and must be treated as such.[5]

Thus was proclaimed his wish to have the rules of international law ignored during the coming campaign. The army lived up to his expectations and, with no particular difficulty, issued two extraordinary directives. According to one, the activity of military tribunals would be suspended during the Russian campaign; local citizens who committed acts of resistance would be summarily executed, while possible excesses on the part of German soldiers would no longer automatically be subject to judicial review. According to the other, communist officials would not be treated as prisoners of war but would be executed immediately after their capture. It could not have been a question here of military security being jeopardized: an entire category of persons was doomed to death on the sole basis of their function.

The army had drastically changed its attitude since the Polish campaign. Hitler's successes constituted one reason; but hatred of communism and contempt for the Slavs, not to mention entrenched anti-Semitic prejudices, provided others. The Army chiefs were none the less happy to leave the implementation of most of Hitler's projected death measures to Himmler. According to an agreement negotiated with Heydrich, the Einsatzgruppen were authorized to carry out, 'on their own responsibility', a purification mission within the army's field of operations. Himmler wanted more, however; he obtained authorization to name 'commanding officers of the SS and the police' (HSSPF) for the rear zones, direct representatives of his power under whose authority troops of the police and the SS, as well as the Einsatzgruppen would be placed.

There are no documents from these first months of 1941 which define the exact nature of the 'special mission' Hitler entrusted to his chief of police. Goering told the head of the department of military armament, on 26 February 1941, that 'like the Führer, he was of the opinion that the entire Soviet Union would collapse at the entry of German troops into Russia'; he added that it would be a matter of 'rapidly liquidating the Bolshevik leaders'.[6] Hitler had grander notions; he spoke of liquidating not only the communist apparatus but also the 'Judeo-Bolshevik intelligentsia'. By this last phrase he meant specifically the Jewish intelligentsia, which comprised, according to him, the core of the Soviet regime. If this interpretation is valid, the mission given to Himmler's troops in Russia would not have differed essentially from what it had been in Poland: the violent destruction of the nation and the annihilation of the ruling class. But the steps taken would be more radical, in so far as the state elite here was confused, in the Nazi mind, with the enemy race.

The only documents referring to the task of the Einsatz-gruppen are signed by Heydrich and dated early in the campaign. The first is a letter of 2 July addressed to the HSSPF, whom Himmler had just appointed.[7] Not having had the opportunity to meet them in Berlin before their departure, Heydrich was communicating the essence of the instructions he had given the Einsatzgruppen. Their mission was to assure the security of the occupied territories. Beyond the usual chores (seizure of archives, establishment of a surveillance and intelligence network, etc.), they were to execute certain categories of persons. The main ones were officials of the communist party, radical elements, and 'Jews occupying positions in the party and in the government' ('Juden in Partei – und Staatsstellungen'). Furthermore, pogoms by the local population should be encouraged and even organized, taking advantage of the chaotic conditions of the early days of the occupation. The other document is dated 17 July, but had been in the planning stage since the end of June. In it Heydrich gave instructions concerning the categories of persons to select for execution among the Soviet prisoners of war, among which were 'all the Jews'.[8]

Neither of these documents refers to, or permits a conclusion about, the existence of an order for the extermination of the entire Jewish population, even though both show that the Nazi attitude had noticeably hardened since the Polish campaign. Nor is there (in my opinion) a valid reason for disregarding the first of them. Granted, Heydrich wrote that he was communicating his orders 'in a condensed form'; but it is very doubtful that he distorted their essential meaning, since the recipients of his letter were being called upon to supervise the operation of the Einsatzgruppen. Could it have been a phony letter, designed for release to the military authorities? Hardly, for Heydrich indicated in it that he had ordered his men to instigate pogroms 'without leaving a trace': he meant to avoid all friction with the military authorities.

Other factors point to the veracity of this document. Heydrich wrote that the immediate goal was to pacify the occupied territories unsparingly. But he added that the final goal, 'upon which the emphasis should be placed', was 'their economic pacification'. In this he was echoing the major concern of Nazi leaders, which was to undertake the exploitation of Russia's resources as soon as possible. No exception concerning the Jews accompanied the mention of this priority. Moreover, in designating as targets 'Jews occupying positions in the party and in the government', Heydrich clearly had in mind the elite of the Jewish population: we recognize the will expressed by Hitler to annihilate the 'Judeo-Bolshevik' ruling class.

The order to foment pogroms shows, on the other hand, that the mission of the Einsatzgruppen went beyond the elimination of a certain social class: the Jewish population was to be indiscriminately assaulted and terrorized during the first days of the occupation. But such an order would make no sense in the context of an extermination plan. There is a world of difference in the thinking behind the covert and rational organization of the genocide and the open use of the most savage violence. Pogroms could only trigger the impulse to flee; a few months later, when the extermination was under way, Heydrich's men, on the contrary, would resort to subterfuge to reassure the Jewish population, to keep it in place or entice it to return, to ensure as complete a massacre as possible. The idea of organizing pogroms can only be understood, finally, in terms of the presumed brief duration the campaign. They were the only means of assaulting the Jews with the manpower available: some 3,000 men for the immense Soviet Union.

Can other sources shed additional light on the subject? Besides Himmler, Heydrich, Goering, and certain high army officials, one other man was intimately involved in the preparation of the campaign, Alfred Rosenberg. Hitler, at the end of March, placed him at the head of a Political Bureau for the Eastern Affairs; on 20 April he confirmed his appointment as chief of the future administration of the conquered territories; and on 17 July he named him Minister for the Eastern Territories. In April Rosenberg wrote down, probably for Hitler's benefit, the goals he considered desirable. Besides 'the complete destruction of the Judeo-Bolshevik governmental administration' and the division of the union into several independent countries, he anticipated certain population shifts, notably in the Baltic states, which were to become part of Germany proper and therefore must be emptied of most of their inhabitants. Rosenberg indicated that the Jews of the region would be resettled, along with other undesirables, in Byelorussia.[9]

In a memorandum dated 29 April, in which he defined the broad outlines of his mission, Rosenberg wrote that the 'Jewish question' called for a comprehensive settlement; in the meantime, a temporary solution would have to be effected which would include such measures as mandatory work and confinement in ghettos.[10] This temporary solution would not lead to extermination but to deportation. In directives dated 3 September and intended for the heads of his administration, he specified once again that the Jewish question would be 'resolved after the war for all of Europe'. Meanwhile, a certain number of measures would have to be implemented, among them the retraining of Jews for agricultural work and the dissemination of Hebrew.[11] For Rosenberg, the resettlement of the Jews in an indeterminate territory always constituted the 'final solution to the Jewish problem'. If an extermination programme for Soviet Jews existed, he obviously knew nothing about it. Would Hitler have entrusted him with such weighty responsibilities and not informed him of a decision of such magnitude, and of such vital concern to him? We shall never know for sure, but it seems unlikely.

Let us turn then to Himmler, whose relationship with Rosenberg was marked from the beginning by defiance and hostility. At the end of May, he approached Bormann for his help in fighting Rosenberg's claim that he would have authority over Himmler in the future conquered territories. On 16 June Bormann wrote to Lammers, the head of the Reich's chancellery, pleading Himmler's cause. He stressed the importance of the mission he would be fulfilling in the east. He added that, 'particularly in the first weeks and months', the police would have to be able to carry out its 'difficult tasks' free of all questions about its competence.[12] Here again, the assumption was that the campaign would be brief, and that Himmler's mission could be completed more or less in the same amount of time.

We do have, furthermore, a noteworthy document on Himmler's views of the future, the famous 'Generalplan Ost'. This is a memorandum which Himmler requested on 24 June from one of his subordinates, and which was sent to him on 15 July, as indicated by the accompanying letter which has survived, unlike the text itself.[13] Its contents are nevertheless known to us through a critical analysis made by an official of Rosenberg's ministry in the spring of 1942.[14] Contrary to what is often asserted, it is highly unlikely that the document under review was a different plan, drawn up by the RSHA at the end of 1941.[15] This 'Eastern Plan' projected the expulsion of several tens of millions of persons – 31 million – from the Eastern territories and the relocation in their place of 4.5 million German settlers. The operation was to be effected over a period of thirty years, with the deportees moving to eastern Siberia.[16]

The population displacements carried out in occupied Poland pale in comparison to what this plan aimed to accomplish. It is a document of special interest regarding the Jews, since the 5–6 million Jews living in the USSR were specifically included in the total of 31 million persons to be expelled.[17] Their fate was not to be extermination but forced resettlement on the other side of the Urals. As the author of the memorandum indicates in his 15 July letter, he had drawn up the plan in accordance with the 'instructions and guidelines' Himmler had given him during their personal talk on 24 June. It is not likely that Himmler would have failed to make his position clear on this point if he had had an extermination plan in mind.

Let us turn finally to Frank. On 19 June Goebbels found himself in Hitler's presence along with Frank, who was discussing the situation in the General Government. Goebbels noted in this regard, 'we are already delighted at the prospect of expelling the Jews'.[18] Frank also believed that the happy event was close at hand. On his return to Cracow, Frank announced that the Führer had expressly told him that the Jews would be leaving the General Government 'in the near future'; as a result, he halted the construction of new ghettos.[19] He had taken Hitler's remarks to be the expression of a seriously intended policy. As is made clear in other documents, he understood that Poland's Jews, and her 'asocial elements' as well, were going to be resettled in the new Lebensraum to the east.[20] On 19 July he wrote to Lammers to request the annexation to the Government General of the Pripet marshes, which he knew to be of scant economic interest, but where he hoped to settle the Jews: by developing this area, they would be performing useful work for the Reich.[21]

Did Hitler envision deporting Europe's Jews to the new territories in the east? Another document seems to confirm it. On 16 August 1941 Antonescu, Romania's Head of State, complained that German troops in the Ukraine were driving back into Romania the Bessarabian Jews that his own soldiers had just pushed to the east. Antonescu asked the Germans to prevent the return of these Jews, a return that 'went against the instructions the Führer had given him in Munich about the treatment of Eastern Jews'; the German troops would simply have to drive them in some other direction.[22] Here it was a question of 'eastern Jews', but it is not impossible that Hitler was thinking of all European Jews. On 22 July he told a Croatian official that he intended to appeal to all European countries to effect the removal of the Jews: whether they were shipped 'to Siberia or to Madagascar was a matter of indifference'.[23]

It is not possible to draw absolute conclusions from all this. Despite the considerable obscurity in which we are left, however, certain points do emerge. No document establishes that Hitler ordered or made plans for the total extermination of the Soviet Jews before the launching of the Russian campaign. Available sources indicate, rather, that the goal remained the expulsion of the Jews from Europe and their concentration in a reservation. Since Madagascar was not feasible in the foreseeable future, Hitler probably envisaged substituting territories to the east. Nothing indicates, in any case, that he had reached a decision; there would be time for that after the campaign, the end of which he thought was close at hand.

The fate awaiting the Soviet Jews can be approached from another angle, by examining the activity of Himmler's troops during the summer of 1941. Historians who speak of an extermination order prior to 22 June base their claim mainly on two sources: the Stahlecker document, which dates from the beginning of 1942 and which will be discussed later, and the testimony of executioners in Nuremberg during the trial of the Einsatzgruppen. In view of the gaps in the documentation, this testimony could not but influence historians. The leaders of the 'intervention groups' were in a good position to know the facts; their depositions agreed.

The principal defendant was Otto Ohlendorf, captain of Group D, and the only one of the four group captains at the start of the Russian campaign to testify; two others were dead and the fourth, Otto Rasch, could not appear in court because of his health. On trial with Ohlendorf were several leaders of the 'intervention commandos' (Einsatzkommandos), the base units (four or five according to the case) into which the groups were subdivided. All these men, with two exceptions, testified that an order to exterminate the Jewish population had been given shortly before the start of the campaign by Bruno Streckenbach, the chief of personnel for the RSHA, on instructions from Himmler and Heydrich. The announcement of this order triggered a general protest and sparked a heated argument with Streckenbach, who cut it off by saying that the order had come from the Führer.[24]

The agreement of the testimony was impressive. It made the deposition of the leader of Commando 5, Erwin Schulz, who stated that he had only heard about the Führer's order several weeks after 22 June, seem like a fluke. The picture would have taken on a different aspect, however, if the other living group captain, Otto Rasch, had been able to appear. Judging from his defence counsel's preliminary statement, it is clear that he would have testified along the same lines as Schulz, whose superior he was: he had not received the Führer's order until several weeks after the start of the campaign, on a date he could no longer specify, some time in August or September.[25]

Today, a certain number of factors which emerged at subsequent trials have led us at least to question, if not to reject, the thesis set forth at Nuremberg.[26] It gave the crucial role to Streckenbach, whose actual duties would not have included it: logically, Heydrich would have issued the order himself. However that may be, Streckenbach, who was believed to be dead by the Nuremberg accused, emerged from a Soviet prison camp in the mid-1950s and denied having given the famous order. Other commando leaders, who until then had eluded the law, also gave testimony in court that failed to confirm the Nuremberg version. Finally, three of the Nuremberg defendants later retracted their statements, saying they had been made under pressure from Ohlendorf who, in the interests of his own line of defence, wanted to appear to have received the extermination order as soon as possible; the role he had played was confirmed by the lawyers of other Nuremberg defendants, including his own.[27]

As they now stand, the testimonies of the first commando leaders tell conflicting stories. With a dozen persons on trial, all pursuing defence strategies to some degree, all struggling with painful memories more or less accurately reconstructed over the decades, this is not surprising. The fact remains that not one of them continues to name Streckenbach as the deliverer of the extermination order, which casts serious doubt on the truth of the Nuremberg depositions.[28] As things stood in 1973,[29] out of ten commando leaders, two claimed never to have received an order to exterminate the Jewish population; one of these, in the past, stated that he had received such an order before the start of the campaign.[30] Four others maintained that they learned of the extermination order after the start of the campaign, one near the end of July, the others in August.[31]

The remaining four stated that the Führer's order was communicated to them before 22 June, and by Heydrich. But they differed as to where this event took place, two locating it in Berlin, the two others in Pretzsch where the groups were formed.[32] But most other testimony indicates that Heydrich only reviewed his troops in Pretzsch. As for the meeting that took place in Berlin in mid-June, Erwin Schulz had given a description of it at Nuremberg which none of his co-defendants contested at the time.[33] According to Schulz, Heydrich had informed them of the imminent outbreak of hostilities and had presented the coming campaign as the battle of two ideologies. Bolshevism would stop at nothing; the Jews would be ruthless enemies who must be struck down more harshly than in Poland. There was no mention of an extermination of the Jewish population.[34]

The testimony is about equally divided on both sides. But the two versions do not equally square with what we know about the way Heydrich's troops fulfilled their mission. Judicial inquiries have, in fact, regularly revealed that victims at first, in the great majority of cases, were men, or at times adolescents. It was only after several weeks, from the beginning of August at the earliest, that women and children began to be systematically slaughtered. That fact is also established in the case of the commandos whose leaders stated they had received the extermination order before the campaign,[35] which raises a question of consistency.

Consider, for example, the account given by Filbert, the leader of Commando 9. The extermination order issued by Heydrich, he testified, was perfectly clear: it extended to the whole Jewish population. But he himself only applied it to men, despite pressure from Berlin, until one day he received a mandatory order to kill women and children also.[36] His subordinates stated that they remembered his communicating this order to them at the end of July. But they also recalled his speaking to them of an 'expansion' and a 'hardening' of the original instructions.[37]

Another example is that of the 'Tilsit' commando, a special unit formed to operate behind the Lithuanian frontier so as to facilitate the work of the other groups and allow them to progress more rapidly toward the East. According to the testimony of the leader of this unit, immediately after the outbreak of the war the head of Group A, Walther Stahlecker, gave him the order to kill all Jews, including women and children, up to twenty-five kilometres beyond the frontier. As the court's investigations brought out, until August the great majority of victims were men. The commando leader asserted repeated pressure from Stahlecker to execute the order as issued; but he denied having complied: Lithuanian collaborators would have started shooting Jewish women and children themselves.[38]

This last statement did not convince the court, but that is not the main point. Like Filbert, the leader of this unit was trying to validate his personal refusal to carry out the order he had been given. However, the order would have been both explicit and issued by an incontestable authority: Himmler himself would have confirmed it in writing. It is obvious that the accused is stretching the point, but still not getting himself out of trouble, the same trouble Filbert was in: if the order had existed as he presented it, he would have carried it out; if he did not do so, it was because such an order did not exist at the beginning. We cannot rule out the hypothesis that an extermination order was issued in a vague or implicit way; this will be discussed later.

Judicial inquiries uncovered a second important factor: the method of execution changed considerably. During the first weeks, the victims were executed according to the provisions of martial law. The firing squads comprised at least as many guns as there were persons in the group to be executed. Death was inflicted by rifle; a volley was discharged at the firing order; in the Tilsit commando, grounds for execution were even given. The victims, who were clothed, were then thrown into ditches.

After a few weeks the SS troops, instead of firing squads, took turns with a submachine-gun and shot to the back of the neck or the head of naked persons kneeling at the edge of a trench or lying in the trench. At first, a layer of dirt was thrown over each row of corpses; soon, the victims were made to lie directly on top of the persons who had just been killed.[39] From military procedure to mass butchery: the methods changed because, after a certain point, the increase in the number of victims meant that everything must be sacrificed to efficiency and speed. But clearly, these developments had been neither anticipated nor rehearsed; as Ohlendorf testified, credibly in this case, there was no instruction or apprenticeship prior to the campaign.[40] The murderers themselves adapted their methods to an eventuality which apparently no one had foreseen.

In view of these factors, the version in which an order was given after 22 June can assume greater credibility, to the degree to which it coincides with actual practice. If we believe the statements of the four commando leaders mentioned above, as well as those of other witnesses, the order to kill Jewish families came several weeks after the invasion of the Soviet Union, some time between the end of July and the end of August. The order came from Himmler, who at various times confirmed it himself during the course of one of his Russian visits, such as the one he made to Minsk in mid-August.[41] It is possible that the order was transmitted at different times to the various groups.

The extermination order was accompanied by considerations that were supposed to justify it. Schulz testified to having been called around 25 July to Jitomir by his group captain, Rasch, who told him that the Jews constituted a mortal danger behind the lines and that the Führer had commanded the liquidation of all Jewish men, in cases where their work was not indispensable. A little later a new order reached Schulz: women and children should also be executed lest they become 'avengers' in the future.[42] Nosske, the leader of Commando 12 who had corroborated Ohlendorf's testimony at Nuremberg, stated in 1971 that he remembered that, about two months after the start of the campaign, Ohlendorf and Rasch had told him about the extermination order; they had discussed the killing of women and children in terms of the elimination of 'potential future enemies'.[43] In Minsk, on 15 August 1941, Himmler declared, after attending an execution during which he felt ill, that the difficult battle the Germans were fighting made such measures necessary; the Jews were the carriers of world Bolshevism, and therefore must be exterminated; the Führer and he himself would answer to history.[44]

All these justifications related, explicitly or implicitly, to the war in progress. The Jews, including women and children, were supposed to constitute a military threat. The argument does not merit discussion, but it has a certain significance. Even for the SS, a justification for the slaughter of women and children was needed: the excuse provided referred to military security; before the start of the campaign, Nazi leaders would have found it difficult to offer such a reason, convinced as they were of a quick, easy victory.

While the version of an escalation by stages of the murders appears to possess greater credibility, credibility is not truth. It remains to examine to what degree the sources of the period confirm or invalidate that version. The activity of the Einsatzgruppen is exceptionally well documented, thanks to the almost daily bulletins issued by the RSHA which collated, sometimes with minor changes, the activity reports of the groups and the commandos. These reports are generally complete and precise; a macabre accounting of the number of victims was kept by each unit.[45]

These reports show that, from the beginning, Heydrich's men carried out executions on a much larger scale than in Poland. Their victims soon numbered hundreds each day. In the beginning pogroms were organized, in accordance with orders, most successfully in the Ukraine and the Baltic states, particularly in Lithuania, whose major cities became the staging grounds for scenes from hell. The groups executed Jews of the male sex almost exclusively; but all Jewish men were not killed. The reports clearly indicate that priority victims were members of the intelligentsia: teachers, lawyers, rabbis, etc., doctors being exempted.[46] Thus in Minsk, all the Jews were assembled in a camp and screened. Only members of the intelligentsia were detained and executed; the others were released and placed in a ghetto.[47]

The Einsatzgruppen created Jewish councils as they passed through an area, decreed laws such as the wearing of an insignia, and established ghettos; the pogroms and executions only did away with a very small proportion of the Jewish population. The groups struck, and then continued their advance, spurred on by Heydrich, who urged them to stay close to the front lines. Speed made them more effective by enabling them to seize valuable archives, to capture communist leaders, and also to take the Jews by surprise. Underlying this urgency was the awareness of a race against time. Heydrich obviously wanted to see his men accomplish as much as possible in the short time they had: on 4 July he called for the formation of an advance-guard commando which was to enter Moscow with the first troops.[48]

In their reports, the groups rarely referred to any orders they might have received; but one document from Group B, dated 5 August, is an exception in this respect.[49] The main thrust of the group's activity 'thus far', we can read, had been directed against the Jewish intelligentsia; Byelorussians had only been executed if they were communists. The mission assigned and accomplished 'thus far' was defined in this way: 'to strike down the Judeo-Bolshevik ruling class in the most efficient manner possible, meanwhile obstructing no more than is strictly necessary the move to place the Russian economy at the service of the German war effort'. These are the same terms and the same concerns set forth in Heydrich's letter of 2 July.

This report confirms, moreover, the reality of an escalation. The phrase 'thus far' ('bisherige') is repeated several times, a phrase that must be correlated with the passage that followed: recently, actions directed against the Jews had 'become more extensive' and passes obtained from the military authorities were 'no longer honoured'. The author of the report made clear, without actually expressing it, the conflict between the mission as it had originally been defined and a new orientation which threatened to sabotage the goal of maximum economic exploitation.

It was only after the beginning of August that indications of a disposition to exterminate appeared. The first is the passage in a report from Commando 10a (Group D) which criticizes the attitude of the Ukrainians who were not prepared to act 'in the direction of a total extermination of the Jews still living here.'[50] In the following weeks and months, we find several indications of the same kind. There was therefore no secret in principle; if the first reports make no mention of extermination, it is because they had no reason to refer to a nonexistent mandate.

Opinions about the 'Jewish question' and how to deal with it are not frequent, but they are revealing. Consider this passage from report of 24 July issued by Group B on the subject of the Jews in Byelorussia: 'A solution to the Jewish question during the war seems impossible in this region since, due to the large number of Jews, it could only be achieved through resettlement.'[51] One senses here the preoccupation with solving the 'Jewish question', as if demands had come from Berlin to think and act along those lines even during the campaign; but the circumspect solution indicates clearly enough that extermination was not yet taken for granted.

A report from Group C, dated 14 August and probably drafted by Rasch, sounds another note. Citing the 'Jewish question', the author stressed the necessity of taking economic realities into account. Until a solution could be achieved on a European scale, the 'surplus Jewish masses' could be used in the reclamation of the Pripet marshes, the Dniepr and the Volga – 'used and exhausted', it was stipulated.[52] It is difficult to interpret this passage other than as the suggestion of an alternative to a decision already made, a solution different in its content but similar in its result: rather than bloody extermination, decimation through work. The idea was raised again in September, in another report from the same group.[53]

The elements mentioned thus far concern all the groups, with the exception of Group A, which operated in the Baltic states. Reports from this group make no reference to the Jewish intelligentsia, giving the impression that from the start its activity was more brutal and less discriminating. In this vein a report informs us that in Dünaburg (Daugavpils) in Latvia, in mid-July, the Jewish men were arrested and executed on the spot, while their families were evicted from the village. No mention was made of selection; the goal seems to have been to empty the city of its Jewish population.[54] We thus cannot exclude the possibility that the group had received special orders.

In fact that is possible, and even probable in the light of Nazi intentions. Unlike the other Soviet territories 'Ostland' (formerly the Baltic states) was to be annexed to the Reich. During a meeting held on 1 August in Rosenberg's presence, the Reich's commissioner for Estonia, Lohse, stated that, in accordance with the Führer's decision, the goal was to Germanize this region; the Jews were to be 'completely removed' from it.'[55] Lohse interpreted this 'removal' as excluding bloodshed. The anti-Jewish agenda he then drafted drew objections from Stahlecker, who, in a document dated 6 August, pointed out that the proposed measures 'were not in accord with the orders given Einsatzgruppe A on the treatment of the Jews in Estonia'.[56] Everything seems to indicate that the orders Stahlecker was referring to at the time were extermination orders. But had this been the case from the beginning?

In early 1942 Stahlecker drew up a document in which he gave an account of his group's activities up to 15 October 1941. This document is often reproduced: with the Nuremberg testimonies, it is the other source that seems to confirm the theory of an extermination order issued before the campaign. In it Stahlecker wrote that, 'in accordance with orders', the security police had decided to resolve the Jewish question 'by every available means and with all due determination'. Further on, he specified that it had been clear, from the start, that the Jewish problem in the Baltic states could not be resolved by pogroms alone. But 'the work of purification' had 'as its goal, in accordance with highest orders, the liquidation of the largest possible number of Jews.'[57]

The possibility cannot be ruled out that Stahlecker was retrospectively giving his mission more scope than it had originally had. But that is not necessarily the case. It is interesting to note that he did not define the order received as the liquidation of all the Jews; he used the expression 'total elimination' further on in his report; but that was to indicate what still remained for him to accomplish. To my mind, the order as he formulates it must be understood in the context of the conditions under which it was given and, more particularly, and again, of the supposed very short duration of the campaign. From this perspective, 'the liquidation of the largest possible number of Jews' did not mean extermination. But it was, by its very formulation, an order whose field of application could only be extended with the prolongation of the war: extermination then would become the extreme.

It is probable that Group A was pressured to act more harshly to free the region as completely as possible from its Jews. In any case, it was not an extermination mission that was being carried out during the first weeks. A report of 11 July from Kowno, a city in the group's jurisdiction, said that 7,800 Jews had been killed, partly by pogroms, partly by executions carried out by Lithuanian collaborators. But the report also announced an end to these mass executions: in future there would be 'smaller executions', of 50 to 100 persons. It was planned to comb through the prisons once again, and also to incarcerate and execute Jews 'whenever there were special grounds'. Furthermore, it was decided with the HSSPF to form a police cordon around Kowno to prevent the return of Jews; the order was given to fire on them 'in case of need'.[58]

No less eloquent is a fragment of a report from early in 1942, most probably drafted by Jäger, the head of Commando 3 and a brute of the first order. 'In the course of the activity' of his commando, he had come to realize that the stabilization of the area behind the front could not be achieved 'by the liquidation of a few Jews'. 'Therefore the Lithuanian territory was cleansed, district by district, of Jews of both sexes,'[59] he notes. Here is confirmation that, at a certain point, a leap was indeed made. Jäger justified it by citing the security requirements behind the front, the Jews supposedly being the partisans' messengers and accomplices. Later, after his indictment, he stated that an extermination order had been issued by Heydrich before the campaign.

The leap shows up even more strikingly in another report, also by Jäger, the only surviving document of its kind.[60] It consists of a compilation of the executions carried out by his commando, day by day, until 1 December 1941. In it the victims are arranged by category and, in the case of Jews, subdivided into men, women, and children. By adding up these numbers we get, for the month of July, a total of 4,239 Jews executed, of whom 135 are women. For August the total climbs to 37,186, the majority (32,430) killed after 15 August, the date on which women and children also began to be murdered *en masse*. The September total reaches a new height: 56,459 Jews killed, of which 15,104 are men, 26,243 women, and 15,112 children. This upsurge could only have come from a political decision which, at a certain moment, made itself unequivocally known.

Jäger's commando was exceptional in its exterminatory activity. But the sudden spurt in executions appears in all the group reports toward the end of August, albeit in varying degrees. Group B announced on 20 August that up to then it had executed 16,964 persons (the great majority of them Jews) and on 28 September, 30,094. Group C, on 20 August, reported a total of 8,000 executions, and 80,000 at the beginning of November. Group D had killed 8,425 persons by 19 August and 35,782 by 30 September. Group A came in first in every instance: by 15 October it had slaughtered close to 120,000.[61] The murderous pressure was strongest in the Baltic region, but the statistical spread is not so great as to require the postulation of a completely different set of orders.

In view of this surge in the killing, we must return to the problem of the initial order. We cannot rule out the possibility that an execution order was given before the campaign; but if so it must have been imprecise or implicit, and this in turn would require explanation. Machiavellianism can still serve as the key: Himmler and Heydrich could have left it up to the heads of the Einsatzgruppen to discern the full implication of the global order they had been issued, thereby giving them time to become inured to the nature of their mission. But this theory overlooks the fact that the campaign was supposed to be short, and that an extermination order, even for Himmler's men, was not the sort of order whose significance can be 'discerned': it would have had to be explicit to be carried out.

This argument supposes, furthermore, that Himmler himself had a firmly fixed intention to exterminate the Soviet Jews. However, his behaviour during the first weeks of the campaign casts serious doubts on this. Enough evidence exists to show that his orders hardened, and that he had not foreseen this murderous escalation. To examine this evidence we must turn away from the Einsatzgruppen, which accounted for only part of the men at his disposal in the Soviet territories. Through the HSSPF, which the army had given him the right to appoint, he also had control over police and Waffen SS troops. After the end of July he involved them in the massacre of the Jews within the framework of operations against the partisans. Several tens of thousands of victims were thereby added to those slaughtered by Heydrich's thugs.[62]

What actual instructions Himmler gave his troops before the campaign remains obscure. They were not, in any case, part of an extermination plan. The judicial inquiry here also revealed that until August, only males had been executed. On 11 July police regiment headquarters transmitted an order from HSSPF headquarters issued by von dem Bach-Zelewski: all Jewish males aged seventeen to forty-five who had been brought to them for acts of looting were to be executed according to martial law. This was an exorbitant penalty. The order was accompanied by additional instructions: the officers were to take special pains with the men assigned to carry out these executions, and make sure they understood the necessity for such a recourse.[63]

Two weeks later, Himmler ordered Bach-Zelewski to organize the pacification of the Pripet marshes. Elements of the Soviet army had dispersed there and posed a threat to the German supply lines. The pacification, as Himmler understood it, was to be total: the enemy was to find in the region neither food nor shelter; all inhabitants suspected of aiding the partisans would be shot, their families evacuated, their dwellings burned.[64] A special fate was reserved for Jews: according to order 42 of the 1st SS cavalry regiment, with the exception of certain qualified workers and doctors, they all would be shot. The justification given was that they supported the partisans and in the future would create pockets of trouble for the German army's rear echelon. On 1 August, Himmler himself specified that all Jewish males must be shot, and women and children 'driven into the marshes.'[65]

At first only those Jewish males arrested for acts of looting were to be executed; then all Jews were transformed into potential partisans: even women and children now deserved to die. Let us note, however, that Himmler had not dared give the order to shoot them. In a report on its activity, the 2nd SS cavalry regiment indicated that the women and children had indeed been driven into the marshes, but without success: the water was not deep enough for drowning to ensue. From the text's reticence, we can conclude that these unfortunates were left alive.[66] During the following weeks the execution of women and children, sometimes in large numbers, as in Kamenets-Podolsk, began to be carried out by Himmler's troops: the final barrier had fallen. At the same time, it became clear that the extermination of masses of people was a backbreaking task.

On 15 August, as we have already seen, Himmler attended an execution in Minsk that upset him. He then asked Nebe, the head of Group B, to find a 'more humane' execution method – more humane for the executioners, since these mass shootings were causing them serious psychic distress. Nebe made a calamitous attempt to use dynamite on mental patients placed in a bunker, then got the idea of harnessing the exhaust fumes from a motor. In the ensuing months, trucks were built by the RHSA with hermetically sealed bodies and a pipe which directed the fumes into the vehicle's interior. A few models of these trucks reached the east near the end of 1941.[67]

If Himmler and Heydrich had known in the spring that their men would be killing women and children in large numbers a few months later, they would have devised less arduous methods than shooting. But nothing had been done; something would have to be invented. The RHSA had made one earlier experiment: in 1940 a truck was used by one of its teams, the Lange Sonderkommando, to kill the mentally ill in East Prussia. But it was, strictly speaking, a gas chamber on wheels: the victims were gassed with canisters of carbon monoxide. The transport of these canisters was difficult over long distances, not to mention costly. The gas truck had been an improvised response to a situation no one had foreseen or imagined. Far from having hoped in some Machiavellian fashion to induce his men to perceive the nature of their extermination mission, Himmler, once he perceived it himself at the same time as they, was only concerned with finding a way to make it less burdensome.

In short, the hypothesis of an extermination order given before the start of the campaign does not stand up to examination. It is, to tell the truth, a highly improbable hypothesis once we reconstruct the perspective of Nazi leaders in the spring of 1941. They could not have been thinking of killing several million people in a few months, much less imagining that the massacre would continue after a speedily won campaign. The army, the administration, and the conservative elite would have had great difficulty condoning the mass execution of civilians, and especially of women and children, once the fighting had stopped.

In all probability, the Einsatzgruppen were told at the beginning of the campaign to kill as many of the Jewish elite as possible, and additionally to strike a deadly blow at the Jewish population by organizing pogroms. An escalation started to occur one month later, which took a decisive turn some time between the end of July and the end of August, when women and children were included in the massacre. The mission of Himmler's troops had been transformed. A rough estimate would show about 50,000 Jews killed up until mid-August, in nearly two months of activity. An impressive figure, ten times higher than the one for Jewish victims of the Polish campaign; but a modest figure compared to the total, ten times higher still, that would be achieved by the end of the year, in four more months. The Jews were paying with their lives, in a geometric progression, for the prolongation of a campaign that should have ended in September.

5

The Final Decision

In August 1941 a catastrophic event began to unfold on the plains of Russia: the extermination of the Jews was leaving the realm of possibility and entering the world of reality. It is conceivable that, from that point on, all Soviet Jews were condemned to die. It is also conceivable that the SS had received an extermination order whose duration and scope were open-ended, and would depend on the subsequent evolution of the campaign. Given the state of our source material, neither of these hypotheses can be proved. We might, however, be able to select one if we can answer a related question: was the slaughter that engulfed Soviet Jews the result of a decision to kill *all* Jews under Nazi control? If genocide had indeed been decreed in the middle of summer, then the policy conducted toward Jews in the Great Reich should have made that apparent.

On 31 July Goering signed a document which completed the mandate he had given Heydrich on 24 January 1939. At that time he had charged Heydrich with achieving the emigration of German Jews; now he was giving him the mission of taking 'all the preparatory steps' necessary to the realization 'of a comprehensive solution to the Jewish question in Germany's zone of influence in Europe'. He asked Heydrich, furthermore, to send him 'promptly' a comprehensive plan of the preliminary measures necessary to the execution of this final solution.[1] It is a document that has become famous, unfailingly quoted whenever the launching of the Holocaust is discussed. And yet it contains nothing that makes it the 'smoking gun'. True, it does date from a time when, in the east, Himmler's thugs were poised to embark on their slaughter of the Jewish population. The hour of death could indeed have come for European Jews. But nothing could be less certain.

The text clearly indicates that it was a question of completing

Heydrich's mandate: completing it by extending its field of application to the whole of Nazi Europe. It also specifies that, to the extent that the jurisdictions of other departments might be infringed upon, they should be consulted and invited to participate. The text identifies the goal of the mandate just as clearly: it was 'to bring to the Jewish question, in the form of an emigration or evacuation, the most constructive solution feasible under the circumstances'.[2] The solutions envisaged were, strictly, emigration and evacuation.

Furthermore, before taking a single step, Heydrich was to submit a comprehensive plan to Goering. Things were therefore at the stage of proposals yet to be approved, not at the final stage of a fully drafted and authorized plan. Finally, Goering's letter only formalized a situation which had existed since the previous summer. Heydrich had been acting since then as if he had jurisdiction over the 'Jewish question' throughout Nazi Europe – notably by sending anti-Jewish advisers to a number of countries.

Just how this text came into being remains obscure. Eichmann wrote in his memoirs that it had been drawn up by his department; Goering had only to sign it.[3] According to a participant in the Wannsee conference, Heydrich stated that he had obtained it from Goering on instructions from Hitler; but the conference's protocol does not confirm the existence of these remarks.[4] The most plausible version is Eichmann's. Heydrich may have wanted authorization in writing in anticipation of the end of the Russian campaign: the realization of the 'final solution' would become the next item on the agenda. Goering's letter proves, in my opinion, that nothing had yet been decided. If Hitler had actually intended to entrust the extermination of the Jews to Heydrich, he would not have troubled to issue a written authorization.

None of the surviving documents from that summer indicates that an extermination had been decided on or prepared for; on the contrary, certain of them allow us to conclude that the projected 'final solution' remained the deportation of the Jews to a reservation. On 1 August, the day after Goering's signature of the famous document, Heydrich wrote to the Minister of Justice, who had sent him a legal proposal for his opinion. It involved introducing, at Hitler's specific request, a penal law that would discriminate against the Jews and Poles still living in the annexed territories. In his reply, Heydrich asked that martial law should apply not only to Poles but equally to Jews. 'Even though we can expect that in the future no Jews will be left in the incorporated territories,' he wrote, it was nevertheless 'urgently necessary in the present situation' to provide for the application of the martial law to them.[5] Obviously he did not think that the disappearance of the Jews was imminent: 'expect that in the future' is a rather vague phrase for someone who supposedly received an extermination order the previous day.

Goering did not seem any clearer about the matter. At the beginning of August, he had had to take a position on putting Jews to work in the Soviet Union. The Jews, he said, 'have nothing more to do in territories occupied by Germany'. For the time being, they should be quartered in barracks and organized into work squads; their food should be the subject of a special regulation and be controlled. Besides, it was doing Jews who had been condemned to death too much of an honour to execute them by firing squad; orders should be given to hang them.[6] All that Goering had to say was that the Jews would be leaving Nazi Europe; he obviously did not know when that would happen. And if their extermination had already been decided upon, he probably would not have felt the need to express himself as he did about their hanging.

The state of things during that summer of 1941 emerges even more clearly when we consider the individuals in the police apparatus directly involved with the organization of the 'final solution': Eichmann, for example, who had hoped to participate in the Russian campaign at the head of an Einsatzkommando. At first disappointed, he later congratulated himself on having escaped a mission that, as he learned from reports received by the RSHA, turned out far differently from how he had imagined.[7] Remaining in Berlin, he would a short time later become a bureaucrat murderer. Meanwhile, on 13 August, he called a meeting at the RSHA of representatives of the Ministry of the Interior, the Four-Year Plan, and the party chancellery.

The immediate purpose of the meeting was to address the problem of half-caste Jews and mixed marriages in Germany: at stake was the deportation of a more or less vast number of persons. Eichmann also had a larger task in mind: he proposed and received support for the creation of an interdepartmental task force that would elaborate a definition of Jewishness on a European scale. It was the first of the 'preliminary measures' concerning which Heydrich had received the go-ahead from Goering. The chief of Jewish Affairs at the Ministry of the Interior saw the danger: in particular, under the pretext of elaborating a definition of a Jew which would be valid for all the territories under German control, were the RSHA and the party not trying to modify the criteria (too generous, according to them) adopted for the Reich soon after the 1935 Congress of Nuremberg?[8]

The real interest in the report of this meeting, however, lies elsewhere. Representatives of the RSHA, the Four-Year Plan, and the party shared the same point of view about half-castes and mixed marriages. In mixed marriages, they were of the opinion that, in a case where the wife was German, she should be 'sent away' ('verschickt') with her Jewish husband and their children. In a case where the man was German, a decision should be made taking three points into account: the value of the individual, possible repercussions on his German relatives, and finally, the concern 'not to supply the Jewish reservoir with any German blood' ('kein deutsches Blut dem Judenreservoir zuführen'). This concern only makes sense if the fate of the Jews to be deported was *not* extermination; according to Nazi concepts, German blood raised the racial level of the Jews. We must conclude from this that, in the minds of the regime's experts, Eichmann at their head, official policy remained, in mid-August, the deportation of Jews to a reservation.[9]

On 3 September an SS officer, Rolf-Heinz Höppner, who was head of the SD and in charge of the relocation of populations in the Wartheland, sent the RSHA a thirteen-page memorandum to which he had put the finishing touches after his 'last conversation' with Eichmann in Berlin. An organization whose task was to deport Jews and Poles to the General Government had existed in the annexed territories since the autumn of 1939. Höppner proposed to expand it to include the whole Reich, and to make it the organ responsible for the deportation which would take place 'after the war' of populations deemed undesirable in the Great Reich; among these he explicitly numbered the Jewish population, within the framework of the 'definitive solution' to the Jewish question.

After having described the structure the new organization should have, Höppner raised the question of the place of destination of these 'undesirable' populations. As he wrote, he did not know the intentions of top officials: he imagined, nevertheless, that the Soviet territory could provide adequate space. But he did not wish to elaborate on the subject as long as 'fundamental decisions' had not been made. All the same, he wished to express a hope: the important thing, from the outset, was to be clear about the fate of the populations to be expelled. Was the goal 'to guarantee them permanently the sure promise of life or was it to exterminate them completely?'[10]

In mid-July Höppner had issued a memorandum on the fate of the Jews in the Wartheland, in which proposals submitted by local police chiefs were reprinted. It was suggested that the Jews of the region be assembled in a large camp and put to work. Since the danger of not being able to feed them all the following winter was real, it should be considered whether 'the most humane solution' might not be to kill those incapable of work by some rapid method. It was furthermore suggested that women of child-bearing age be sterilized, thus resolving the Jewish problem for the next generation. In a letter to Eichmann accompanying the memorandum, Höppner wrote that, although the options mentioned might seem 'in part fantastic', in his opinion they were perfectly feasible.[11]

It is not surprising that the SS leaders in the Wartheland came to the idea of extermination sooner than the others: the Jews had been a burden to them for almost two years. Their suggestions were not taken up immediately, however. In his September memorandum, Höppner had noted that 'fundamental decisions' had not been made. But his awareness of the atmosphere, and the knowledge he must have had of the activities of the Einsatzgruppen, had impelled him to request clarification on the fate of 'undesirable' populations: survival or death? The reply would come soon afterwards; but at the beginning of September the men who would be the first executioners in the genocide still had the deportation of the Jews to an undetermined territory as their long-term goal.

Emigration remained open to Jews, for that matter, even though a new restriction had been enacted in August. It was now illegal for Jews of arms-bearing age, that is, between the ages of eighteen and forty-five, to emigrate.[12] The great majority of the Jews who had stayed in the Reich were old; the young had been the first to leave; but it is

interesting to note this preoccupation of the Nazis, quick
to see the Jews as potential enemy combatants. Meanwhile
emigration continued to be encouraged, as the head of the
Gestapo emphasized in a circular dated 21 August.[13] A few
thousand Jews were therefore able to emigrate during 1941,
despite war-related obstacles.

In July and August, the only death preparations made in
the Reich by Himmler's department were not intended for the
Jews, but for Soviet functionaries. According to the RSHA,
the army only partially fulfilled the order to kill political
functionaries, instead dispatching them to the rear with
other prisoners of war. Heydrich received permission to
send commandos to make selections in the prisoner-of-war
camps; for reasons of secrecy, the persons chosen were to
be executed in the nearest concentration camp. Some time
in July or August, at the camp in Sachsenhausen, north of
Berlin, a meeting took place in the presence of Eicke, the
Inspector of Camps, who announced the imminent arrival
of 18,000 Soviets and demanded the development of a fast
method for killing them.

A facility was soon completed, one which the other camps
would imitate. In the guise of a medical visit, the Soviets were
led one by one into a room and placed under a measuring
device containing, at neck-level, a hole through which a pistol
shot could be fired. Between the beginning of September and
mid-November, at least 6,500 Russians were murdered in this
fashion.[14] In September at Auschwitz, other Soviet prisoners
were killed by gassing with the aid of a powerful disinfectant,
Zyklon B; the process continued to be used on a small scale
during the following months, before being used on a massive
scale for killing Jews.[15]

For the time being, the Jews of the Reich endured the usual
persecution. Two new measures, however, came to seal
their doom: in August they were forced to wear a badge;
in September their deportation to the east was ordered.
These two decisions came from Hitler himself, who in both
cases reversed his earlier position. At the end of 1938 he
had refused to impose a distinctive insignia on the Jews;
subsequently, the measure had only been introduced in the
eastern territories. In August 1941 Goebbels, still obsessed
by the Jews' presence in Berlin but also alarmed by the
situation on the eastern front, persuaded himself that the

'Jewish question' had 'again become acute'. Soldiers home on leave, he wrote, must no longer be confronted with the spectacle of Jews employing German domestics, enjoying large apartments, or hoarding provisions vital to the Aryan population. Identification must be imposed on them, which would keep them from spreading defeatist rumours and lowering morale.[16] On 15 August a meeting was hastily called at the Ministry of Propaganda. The experts on Jewish affairs from the other ministries were brought up to date on Goebbels' proposal and asked for their support. Eichmann, who represented the RSHA, informed the assembly that Heydrich had recently addressed a request of the same nature to Goering; since he had replied that only the Führer could make such a decision, a new proposal was being drawn up for submission to Hitler.[17]

Goebbels got ahead of Heydrich. Received by Hitler on 18 August, he submitted his proposal, which was accepted. The wearing of an insignia would eliminate the danger of Jewish 'bellyachers and defeatists' going unrecognized.[18] The measure was basically linked to the state of the war, to the difficult struggle unfolding on the eastern front, and to its possible repercussions on the morale of the German population. Goebbels knew that he would strike a sympathetic chord in Hitler. During the First World War, had not the danger within come from the demoralizing activity Jews were freely able to exercise on the home front?

On 1 September came a public proclamation that all Jews over six years old must wear a yellow star sewn onto their clothing. Was this the beginning of the end? Nothing allows us to think so. Such a measure was indeed a preliminary condition for an eventual deportation, but it was not adopted in view of an impending deportation. At the time of the 15 August meeting at the Ministry of Propaganda, Eichmann had also informed those present about the RSHA's evacuation plans. Heydrich had submitted a detailed proposal to the Führer, who had rejected any evacuation during the war. Another project was now under study, which envisioned a partial evacuation of large cities.[19] Nothing was said about the destination of these deportations; in view of the situation, it could only have involved the Soviet Union.

During his interview with Hitler on 18 August, Goebbels had also asked for authorization to deport the Berlin Jews. Hitler replied that he would be able to send them to the east immediately after the end of the campaign.[20] Since the summer of 1940, his response had invariably been that the deportation of the Jews would take place after the war. He was now ready to consider their deportation to the east even before the war with Britain was over; but in any eventuality such action would have to await the end of the eastern campaign. At the beginning of September German military authorities in Serbia sought to deport 8,000 Jewish men from the region, on the pretext of halting spreading partisan activity. To a request of the Ministry of Foreign Affairs concerning the eventual deportation of these Jews to the General Government or Russia, Eichmann answered on 13 September that it was out of the question: even Jews from the Reich could not be sent there.[21]

A few days later, on 18 September, Himmler wrote from the Führer's headquarters to Greiser, the Gauleiter of the Wartheland, to inform him of an event that represented a radical change of attitude on Hitler's part. The Führer now wished the Reich and the protectorate of Bohemia-Moravia to be liberated 'as rapidly as possible' from all resident Jews. Himmler announced his intention of completing this mission even before the end of the year. As a first step, he proposed to transport the Jews to the annexed territories before deporting them the following spring 'further to the east'. He asked Greiser to accommodate 60,000 persons in Lodz for the winter and said that Heydrich, who would be in charge of the operation, would get in touch with him.[22]

Nothing is indicated about the motivation for this volte-face, which Hitler must have revealed to Himmler that same day, 18 September, or the day before at the earliest. One possible line of thought would lead to Rosenberg who, on 14 September, charged his liaison officer at the army's high command, Otto Bräutigam, with submitting the following proposal to Hitler: the USSR had just announced the deportation of Germans from the Volga; in reprisal, the Jews of Central Europe should be deported to the East. Bräutigam was able to reach Hitler's Wehrmacht adjutant, Schmundt, who told him that 'it was a very pressing and important option which greatly interested the Führer'. The next day he learned that Hitler had ordered that the Minister of Foreign Affairs's opinion be sought first.[23] The matter then seemed to sink like a stone. Rosenberg's liaison officer at the Führer's headquarters wrote on 21 September that

Hitler had still not come to a decision; it is true that he only learned on 7 October of the order to deport Jews to the east, and also that, according to his information, this order only involved the Jews in the Protectorate.[24] It is possible, then, that Rosenberg's proposal played a part in Hitler's decision to deport the Jews even though the campaign was not over; but in any case, it can only have been a minor part.

What was the meaning of this decision? Had it been made in the context of reprisals, with no view to a general massacre? Or did it mean that the hour of extermination had come? A great deal of what happened during those crucial weeks of September and October remains obscure; but a series of converging facts make the second interpretation more convincing.

On 4 October Heydrich had a conversation with Rosenberg's aide-de-camp, Gauleiter Meyer. The Jewish question was one of the subjects broached. Heydrich wondered if Rosenberg's ministry 'still' had to keep its own chargés d'affaires for Jewish matters; his hope was that the SS would have a monopoly. The interesting thing, however, is in a point raised in a report on the meeting, a point that was not necessarily discussed with Meyer. A 'danger' was highlighted: numerous businesses would want to keep their Jews on the pretext that they were indispensable and no one would take the trouble to train replacements. 'But this would reduce to naught the plan for a total resettlement of the Jews out of the territories occupied by us.'[25]

Leaving aside the pomposity ('reduce to naught') which betrays the fanaticism of the RSHA men, this comment is remarkable. It shows that they were then only at the very beginning of a vast operation: it was still just a project whose accomplishment, it was feared, would run into serious obstacles. It seems, furthermore, that this project involved all the territories under the Reich's control. In his letter to Greiser, Himmler mentioned only the Jews of the Reich and the Protectorate: perhaps he did not wish to frighten his correspondent by raising the prospect of the arrival of Jews from all over Nazi Europe; perhaps the plan was expanded shortly afterwards. In any case, could this 'resettlement' have been anything other than extermination? Heydrich included the Soviet Jews in the 'plan' in question: where on earth could they be resettled in the middle of a war? And what fate, if not death, would await Jews who would be sent from all over Europe to a region where the Jewish population was already being indiscriminately massacred?

Two days earlier, during the night of 2 October, seven Parisian synagogues were damaged by bombs; several Frenchmen and two German soldiers were wounded. Asked by the occupying authorities to clarify the matter, Heydrich's representative in France, Helmut Knochen, replied that it was a purely French affair, and that those guilty of the bombings very probably belonged to anti-Semitic factions of the collaboration. As a result of a leak, it became clear that the information Knochen had released suffered from a considerable omission: the bombings had indeed been committed by Frenchmen, members of Eugenè Deloncle's collaborationist group; but their explosives had been supplied by Knochen's own men. At this news the German military commandant, Otto von Stülpnagel, flew into a rage and wrote to Berlin demanding Knochen's recall.[26]

In a letter he sent the army high command (OKH) on 6 November, Heydrich assumed full responsibility for the affair. After the wave of attacks on the German army and on French politicians favourable to the collaboration (Laval and Déat had been wounded during an assault on 29 August), Deloncle had volunteered to organize reprisals against the Jews. Heydrich accepted his offer, but stated that he had done so 'only from the moment when, at the highest level, Jewry had been forcefully designated as the culpable incendiary in Europe, one which must definitively disappear from Europe'.[27]

If these words have a meaning, it is that the deportation order had been, simultaneously, an extermination order. The indirect reference to Hitler ('at the highest level') would have no purpose if the 'disappearance' of the Jews were to be an innocent affair. Heydrich also confirms for us that the order had been given in September, probably in the latter half of the month: one or two weeks would have sufficed for organizing the reprisals. We shall also bear in mind the motive put forward to justify the 'disappearance' of the Jews: they were 'incendiaries' – in Hitlerian language, the perpetrators of the war, those who lit the gunpowder and fanned the flames, spreading the fire to the whole world.

The tone of his letter, like his behaviour throughout the incident, gives the impression that Heydrich felt exalted by the mission he had been given. In any event, he must have been very sure of his position to embark on such an endeavour, one which risked a clash with the army. He wrote, incidentally, that he was 'completely aware of the political implications' of the steps he had taken, since he had been entrusted 'for years with administering the final solution to the Jewish question in Europe'. Something had happened, then, which explained his action. It was not immaterial, finally, that he chose Paris as his target. The reprisals would notify the Jews, 'once so powerful in Paris', that they could no longer feel safe in the country which until then had been their 'European centre'. The destruction of the Paris synagogues was a death notice, the symbolic announcement of the annihilation to come.

In Jerusalem, Eichmann stated that he was informed of an order to exterminate the Jews 'two months' or 'three months' after the start of the war against the Soviet Union. Summoned by Heydrich, he heard him speak this sentence, without at first grasping its import: ' "The Führer has ordered the physical destruction of the Jews." . . . He spoke that sentence to me. And as if he then wished to observe the effect of his words, quite contrary to his custom, he paused for a long while. I can still remember it today.'[28] Eichmann was not able to be more precise about the date on which this conversation took place. He testified that on the same day Heydrich sent him to inspect the extermination preparations being made in Lublin by Globocnik, the regional head of the police and the SS. He recalled having seen men sealing wooden barracks to make them airtight; Jews were to be gassed inside them by means of a high-powered diesel motor. The facility he was describing could only have been Belzec; but work did not start there until the end of October or the beginning of November, which would place his visit some time in November or December. Eichmann had probably telescoped two distinct events in his mind.[29] As we shall see, there is every reason to think that he was fully aware of the extermination project by the end of September.

At that point he was busy organizing the deportation of some of the German Jews to Lodz. On 29 September he succeeded in obtaining the go-ahead from the Minister of the Interior, by means of alleging that the Lodz authorities had endorsed the planned deportation – which was a lie. The administrative head of the province of Lodz, Friedrich Übelhör, a high-ranking honorary SS officer,

actually opposed the resettlement of tens of thousands more
Jews in an already overcrowded ghetto. He expounded his
views at great length to Himmler, laying the blame on the
cavalier behaviour of Eichmann, whom he called a 'gypsy
horse trader', an insult poorly tolerated in SS circles. In
this well-known exchange of letters,[30] which ends with a
curt reprimand from Himmler, there is a neglected and yet
highly interesting piece of information.

In his letter of 9 October Übelhör wrote that for several
days the local Gestapo had been working on the reorganization of the Lodz ghetto, which was to be split into
two strictly separate sections. One was to become a work
ghetto ('Arbeitsghetto'), where the some 40,000 working
Jews would be concentrated. The other would be a 'maintenance ghetto' ('Versorgungsghetto'), where all Jews who
did not work, at the time about 100,000 persons, would live.
Übelhör raised vigorous objections to this project, pointing
out that factories were scattered throughout the ghetto and
that it would be impossible to concentrate all the Jews
incapable of work in the space provided by the Gestapo;
the second ghetto was to cover an area of 0.748 km^2, as
opposed to the 3.162 km^2 allotted for the first.[31] There is
no question about the meaning of this reorganization: the
division of the ghetto would permit the preservation of Jews
who could work: the others would be killed. It is virtually
certain that Eichmann, who maintained close ties with the SS
leader in charge of Jewish questions in Lodz, was involved in
this reorganization.

At the same time, preparations for extermination were
getting under way in the region. SS officer Herbert Lange,
who worked for the Posen Gestapo and had massacred the
mentally ill during the preceding year, received the order to
set up the necessary installation. Accompanied by an aide,
he made several tours of the Warﾃheland in search of an
appropriate site, then returned to Berlin and reported to the
RSHA.[32] At the end of October a commando unit moved into
the little town of Chelmno and built a camp there. Two gas
trucks, furnished by the RSHA, arrived soon after; in early
December the local Jews were gassed; in January it was the
turn of the inactive Jews of the Lodz ghetto.

Was the extermination of the Jews in the Wartheland an
ad hoc operation, a way for Greiser to get rid of a population
that was overburdening him? We can imagine him making

some sort of deal with Himmler, accepting new Jews in return for permission to kill off his inactive Jewish population. In a letter to Himmler dated 1 May 1942, Greiser recalled, of the extermination of 100,000 Jews of his region, that it had been 'authorized' by Himmler – as if the proposal had come from someone else, i.e. from Greiser himself.[33] This is quite possible, but it should not lead us to conclude that the extermination of the Jews started in a localized fashion, later expanding and becoming generalized.[34] For at the same moment, further east in the Lublin area, preparations were also being made to exterminate the Jews of the General Government.

The men in charge here were Bouhler's crew from the Führer's chancellery, who had found themselves released from their 'euthanasia' mission. On 24 August Hitler had ordered a halt to the operation; the Bishop of Münster's public protest, coming after other outcries, apparently made him fear demonstrations that would be ill-timed, occurring just when the war in the east demanded solid popular support for the regime. Did he have another job in mind for the 'euthanasia' crews? It does not seem so. According to Victor Brack's testimony at Nuremberg, a large number of employees were dismissed after the suspension of the operation.[35] A few weeks later, apparently after a conversation between Bouhler and Himmler,[36] came an unexpected assignment: part of the remaining personnel were sent to work for Globocnik in Lublin. Brack and Bouhler visited him themselves in September, according to Brack.[37] Captain Christian Wirth, a 'euthanasia' veteran who would oversee all the extermination camps in the General Government, was also placed at Globocnik's disposal 'late in the summer of 1941.'[38] At the end of October he began construction of the Belzec camp. All of this points to a central decision, which must have dated back to the end of September or the beginning of October.[39]

While the extermination machinery was still under construction, the RSHA moved ahead with the deportations. It was not possible to wait until everything was ready; the Reich had to be 'liberated' from its Jews as soon as possible; the first trains began to roll towards Lodz on 16 October. A few days earlier, on 10 October, a meeting had taken place in Prague chaired by Heydrich, who had been ordered by Hitler at the end of September to bring the Protectorate, which had been growing restless, back under control. Eichmann was present, along with the highest local officials of the police and the SS. They were reminded that the Führer wished to have the Jews gone from 'German space' by the end of the year; nothing must stand in the way, not even transportation problems. We feel here, once again, that the SS was aware that it was embarking on a historic task.

Lodz and the difficulties encountered there were also brought up. Probably following a discussion between Greiser and Himmler, Lodz ultimately only had to accommodate 20,000 Jews and 5,000 gypsies, instead of the 60,000 persons originally scheduled. The RSHA, as a result, had to look for other destinations. As we learn from the minutes of this meeting, Riga and Minsk were chosen, cities in the area of operations of the Einsatzgruppen. Eichmann mentioned the possibility that Jews might also be sent to the 'camps for communist prisoners' of groups B and C. No use wondering what might be the fate of all these people, especially in light of the following detail: the 50,000 Jews earmarked for Riga and Minsk were to be chosen from among 'the most onerous', in other words, the infirm, the sick, and the inactive.[40] From 14 November a series of trains departed for the Soviet Union: most of the passengers were shot upon arrival.

Other proposals entertained in the course of this meeting indicate that it was indeed extermination that was now on the agenda. Thus, it was provided that Jews from the Protectorate would be grouped in two ghettos which themselves would be divided into a work ghetto and a maintenance ghetto. It was expected that the Jews would emerge 'already heavily decimated' ('ja schon stark dezimiert') even before their evacuation to the east. It was recommended, moreover, to proceed with caution in the case of Jews who had influence in high places; this was to limit as much as possible any interventions that might be made on their behalf.[41] The problem was seriously considered; on 1 November Himmler noted, after a telephone conversation with Heydrich, 'place for Jews over sixty years old;'[42] plans for a showcase ghetto, such as the one that would be established in Theresienstadt, were taking shape.

All that remained was to tighten the net. On 2 or 3 October Himmler, who was in Kiev, had Eichmann flown in so that he could give him a comprehensive report on the state of Jewish emigration.[43] On 18 October he noted, after a telephone conversation with Heydrich: 'no overseas emigration of Jews'. Five days later, the head of the Gestapo informed his departments that the emigration of Jews was now prohibited.[44]

Everything had been orchestrated in the space of four weeks, from 18 September to 18 October. The Wannsee meeting would only record a solution already reached in mid-October by Himmler and his men. This solution had been reached by piecing together several disparate elements: the experience in deportation matters accumulated by the RSHA since the autumn of 1939; the death techniques developed separately, and for other, or more limited, purposes by the Führer's chancellery and Heydrich's men in the Soviet Union; finally, the distinction between active and inactive Jews that had become current in official circles of the ghettos of Poland.

Trial and error had been reduced to a minimum. The dispatching of Jews to the Soviet Union was primarily due to the pressure exerted by a Hitler desirous of 'purifying' the Reich by the end of the year, even though extermination sites were just starting to be built. Furthermore, it seems that at the time police officials were thinking about setting up camps in the USSR. Heydrich told Goebbels, whom he met at Hitler's headquarters on 23 September, that, as soon as the military situation permitted, the Jews would be transported to camps built by the communists along the White Sea canal.[45] Whether or not these projects were actually considered, they had to be rapidly abandoned. The death camps were eventually concentrated in the General Government and in Upper Silesia.

From mid-October 1941 the circle of the initiated would widen. On 23 October an editor at *Stürmer*, Streicher's anti-Semitic newspaper, already knew that in the east 'special measures' were being adopted, thanks to which 'a large part of the Jewish vermin' would be exterminated in the near future.[46] On 25 October the man in charge of Jewish affairs in Rosenberg's ministry wrote to Lohse, the Reich's commissioner for the Ostland, to inform him that Brack had said he was ready, with Eichmann's approval, to furnish 'gassing equipment' to kill Jews unable to work. Eichmann had furthermore announced that the Reich's Jews would be deported to the East, and that those who were able to work would be employed there.[47]

In September Frank still hoped that the Jews would be deported 'to refuges in deepest Russia (Ural)'.[48] On 13 October he told Rosenberg that he wished to ship the Jews of the General Government to the East; Rosenberg answered that that was impossible for the time being, but that he would do his utmost, when the time came, to achieve this resettlement.[49] Rosenberg must have been informed of the extermination programme soon afterwards, in mid-November at the latest. On 18 November, at a press conference, he stated confidentially that the 'Jewish question' could only be resolved 'by the biological extermination of all the Jews in Europe'.[50] Two days earlier Goebbels had published an article in the newspaper *Das Reich* in which he wrote that Hitler's prophecy was coming true. Frank himself was probably informed near the end of November, after having sent one of his aides to Berlin; on 16 December, in any case, he told his close associates of the coming massacre.[51]

In early November Eichmann began preparing for an inter-ministerial meeting on the 'Jewish question'. On 29 November invitations went out for 9 December; probably because of the Japanese attack on the United States, the meeting was postponed until 20 January 1942. There was no need to rush: the meeting aimed at getting the ministerial bureaucracy to endorse an operation that was already under way. The minutes, written by Eichmann, were also edited by Müller, the head of the Gestapo, and by Heydrich himself. Everything must not be told, but the main point must emerge; Heydrich wished, according to Eichmann, to register the approval given his task by this assembly of government officials.[52] The final document said nothing about the fate reserved for Jews unfit to work. But it is easy to grasp in the light of what awaited the others: a large number of those able to work would die as they worked; survivors would be killed so that the Jewish peril would never arise again.[53]

Nazi leaders seem to have seriously contemplated utilizing Jews capable of working. The manpower crisis was probably the reason. Himmler, by the end of September, had made clear his intention to assign productive work to concentration camp inmates.[54] Able-bodied Jews were to make their contribution to the economic empire he aspired to build. Very few would do so, in the end: the extermination machinery slaughtered able-bodied Jews along with the rest. We cannot construe this as a further escalation of the killing, however: Jews capable of work had only been granted a stay of execution as it was.

6

Hitler and the Genocide

Two major turning-points have emerged in the actions of those who executed anti-Jewish policy: the first during August 1941, when the massacre of Jews in the Soviet Union assumed the dimensions of a genocide, the second around the middle of September, when the decision to deport the Jews of the Great Reich to the east was accompanied by preparations indicating that all Jews under Nazi control would henceforth be marked for death, either immediate or deferred. A full month passed between these two turning-points; the surge in killings in the Soviet Union, therefore, did not mean that the matter had been definitively settled. Everything seems to suggest that there was a decision-making process lasting several weeks before the fatal verdict was handed down in September.

It was on the Führer's authority that Himmler ordered his troops to exterminate women and children in the Soviet Union. It was unquestionably Hitler who decided that the Reich Jews should wear a yellow star, and then that they would be deported to the east; and there is no reason to doubt that it was he who gave the order to commence preparations for the genocide. Still, there is nothing to enlighten us about the reasons that led him to these decisions, or about his manner of presenting them to his lieutenants. Perhaps something will emerge, however, if we reconstruct the context in which these decisions were made. The way Hitler perceived the progress of the Russian campaign, how he reacted to it, and the ensuing repercussions on his plans for the Jews – all this will permit us to fill in the picture and verify the interpretation proposed in this work.

One might at first glance question the validity of this interpretation. At the end of the summer of 1941 the Reich was at the peak of its territorial expansion, and only four long years of hard fighting would bring it to its knees. The conflict had not yet become global; that would not happen until December, with the Japanese attack on Pearl Harbor and Germany's declaration of war on the United States. But our retrospective view of the Second World War is deceptive: we must focus on Hitler's perception of things at the time. In this respect, the documentation is sufficiently abundant to illuminate the context in which the shift toward genocide took place.

The Russian campaign was planned in an atmosphere of unprecedented confidence. The German army, which until then had gone from victory to victory, would make short work of an enemy that was poorly equipped, poorly led, and minimally motivated. At least, that was how the German leaders saw things. Rosy estimates about the state of Soviet rearmament, deeply rooted prejudices about the Slavic ability to organize, and equally entrenched notions about the unpopularity of the Stalin regime: these all pointed to optimism. Capitalizing on its power and mobility, the German army would surround the Soviet troops and crush them before they had time to retreat. The immediate result of this massive strike would be the collapse of the enemy regime.

The projected duration of this new blitzkrieg ranged from a few weeks to a few months, according to the greater or lesser optimism of those in charge. The army high command set the date at mid-September.[1] In June, Hitler spoke to Goebbels of a four-month war; the latter was surprised: he was convinced it would be shorter, that 'Bolshevism would topple like a house of cards'.[2] Hitler was one of the moderate optimists; suspicious by nature, he was quick to conjure up unforeseen difficulties. He knew that everything hinged on speed, and that nothing must jeopardize it. On 17 March 1941 he told the army chief of staff, Franz Halder: 'We must have early successes. There must be no reversals.'[3]

The Russian campaign was a gamble, and Hitler knew it full well. In the weeks preceding 22 June, he ceaselessly fretted over its perils and promises. Operation Barbarossa represented 'a risk',[4] and even 'a big risk'.[5] He had the feeling of standing 'outside a closed door' which led to the unknown: would he be confronted by 'secret weapons', or by 'the tenacity of fanatics'?[6] It was 'a difficult undertaking'. 'If it went wrong, then, one way or another, all would be lost.'[7] On the other hand, he had confidence in his army, and thought the war with England would soon be over. The defeat of the Soviet Union would induce her to give up the fight, perhaps even before the end of the year.[8]

So many things depended on the success of Barbarossa. Germany had to place herself in a position to end the war with England, or to wage it against the allied Anglo-Saxon powers if necessary. She also had to strengthen an economy which had not been mobilized for a long war and was showing signs of serious stress, especially in the areas of manpower and raw materials. Another reason for a short campaign: limited destruction would permit a rapid exploitation of Russia's resources.

Once the USSR was beaten, it was anticipated that in the autumn the German army would engage in campaigns in the Near East, seal off the Mediterranean by seizing Gibraltar, and occupy West Africa and the Atlantic islands. Great Britain then would be forced to make peace, at the latest in 1942. For its part, Japan, freed from Soviet pressure, would no longer hesitate to seize British possessions in the Far East, by the same token keeping the United States at bay. American intervention remained Hitler's major preoccupation. Without it, he thought, the war would be over by the end of the year; with it, the fighting would continue 'for years to come'.[9]

The first weeks of the campaign fulfilled his fondest hopes. The enemy front was easily penetrated, and the German armies advanced at top speed deep into Soviet territory. Day after day the plunder was announced with great fanfare: enormous quantities of material, hundreds of thousands of prisoners. By the beginning of July the German generals viewed the campaign as virtually won.[10] Hitler gave free rein to his dreams of colonization, revealing the brutal conception he had of that war. On 8 July he announced that he would pulverize Moscow and Leningrad with his air force. In this way he would lose neither men nor tanks, nor would he have to feed their populations in the coming winter. He heartlessly pictured the approach of a demographic catastrophe that would sap the vital forces not only of Bolshevism but of the Russian people itself.[11]

His anti-Semitic obsession evidently had not left him, erupting in the middle of military operations. On 10 July he showed the greatest anxiety about the armoured divisions headed for Kiev; he was sure the bridges would be destroyed, since 35 per cent of the city's inhabitants were Jews.[12] In his eyes they could only be active, ruthless adversaries. And yet the concept of a massacre still seemed far from his mind. At the end of the same day, he declared to a small group that in politics he was the equivalent of Robert Koch in bacteriology. Just as Koch had exposed the bacillus as the cause of tuberculosis, so he had unmasked the Jew as the 'ferment of social decay'. He had proved that a country could live without Jews: this was 'the worst blow' he had dealt them.[13]

On 14 July he approved the armament programme that was to take effect at the end of Barbarossa. The total strength of the army would be substantially reduced, thereby allowing one million workers to return to production; at the same time, the number of armoured divisions would be multiplied to permit the successful completion of the operations planned for the Near East and North Africa. But it was the air force that was to be the chief beneficiary of the new arms effort, a crucial weapon in the final show-down with Great Britain.[14] The adoption of this programme proves that, in Hitler's eyes, the first weeks of the campaign had lived up to his expectations. And yet many doubts had assailed him.

As early as 30 June he had expressed to Mussolini his surprise at discovering the great quantity of armaments the enemy had at its disposal.[15] Soon he was obliged to acknowledge that the number of reserves also had been grossly underestimated. But most striking were the combativeness and tenacity displayed by the Soviet troops; a morale that would stiffen once they became aware of the fate awaiting their political leaders and the treatment of prisoners of war in general, not to mention the occupying army's policy of random reprisals. In the West, meanwhile, the situation had also deteriorated: on 7 July the United States established a military base in Iceland. Once again Hitler resisted pressure from his navy: he wanted to delay an American entry into the war 'for one or two months'; by that time victory in the east would probably have a deterrent effect on the attitude of the United States.[16]

On 15 July he received the Japanese ambassador, Oshima. He disclosed to him 'the series of surprises' he had just encountered in terms of the Soviets' 'gigantic' supplies of armaments and their fierceness in battle: the Russians fought 'like wild animals'. He nevertheless estimated that the conflict would be over by the middle of September. His optimism was no doubt largely sincere, but also served a purpose: after urging Japan all spring to attack British possessions in the Far East, Hitler now hoped she would enter the war against the USSR. He had no need of assistance, he assured the ambassador; he was only thinking of the common future of Germany and Japan. He did admit, however, that it would be easier to beat the Soviet Union with a joint action. A speedy defeat in this area, he emphasized, was in the interests of both countries: it would keep the United States out of the war.[17] An anxiety was being expressed here, or at least a concern, which others also felt. Thus in Rome, on 9 July, Ciano noted that the German army was advancing at a slower pace because of the stubborn resistance of the Russians; and on the 16th he reported Mussolini's fear that the Reich would not be victorious before winter, at which point many unknown factors would come into play.[18]

During the last two weeks in July, anxiety gradually assumed crisis proportions. Despite enormous losses the enemy kept on fighting fiercely, and new divisions continued to appear. It became increasingly clear that, despite the victories achieved and the territory conquered, the German army had not attained its objective. The Soviet combat force had been decisively weakened, Halder estimated on 23 July, but it had not been destroyed.[19] The enemy had been able to protect an important part of its troops from encircling operations; it was now in a position to reorganize its defences with growing effectiveness. On 25 July the commander-in-chief of the army, Brauchitsch, spoke of the Soviet army as the 'first serious adversary', adding that 'the length of the war wore at the nerves'.[20]

Hitler, too, became obsessed by the time it was taking. Keitel reported on 25 July that the Führer was asking himself 'with apprehension: "how much time do I have left to finish off Russia, and how much time do I still need?" '[21] Goebbels experienced the same apprehension; his diaries show how quickly the horizon had darkened. On 17 July he noted with mounting concern 'the enemy's extraordinarily strong resistance on all fronts'.[22] Two days later, he described the war as a struggle for survival between Bolshevism and Nazism.[23] On 26 July he decided to issue new instructions regarding propaganda: 'The people must know that Germany now is fighting for her life and that we must choose between the total annihilation of the German nation and domination of the world.'[24]

The doubt that had seized Hitler showed in his behaviour. The initial plan of attack had been frustrated by the enemy's unexpected resistance, but no provisions had been made for this eventuality. War directive no. 33, which he issued on 19 July, triggered a long month of quarrels with his military advisers, particularly with Halder, about what strategy to pursue next. While the army chief of staff urged him to deploy his forces toward Moscow and destroy the bulk of the Soviet army there, he wanted to advance along its flanks, eventually surrounding Moscow from behind, but in the meantime capturing the industrial centres and sources of raw materials in northern Russia and the Ukraine. Conflicting instructions resulted from these acrimonious disputes. On 30 July the pivotal decision was simply delayed: for the time being, owing to the approach of significant enemy forces and the need for supplies and repairs to the armoured divisions, the group of armies located at the central front received the order to go on the defensive.[25]

The adversities encountered since mid-July took their toll on Hitler's state of mind, notably on his concept of maintaining order and on his attitude toward the Jews. On 3 July Stalin had called upon the Soviet people to conduct guerrilla warfare against the rear echelons of the German army. The limited reserve troops of the latter were mobilized against a danger that was still negligible, but that would grow in direct ratio to the extraordinarily brutal repression that was used to subdue it. On 16 July, during a meeting of the principal Nazi leaders, Hitler spoke of the goals of the war in the east. He intended to keep the conquered territories and treat them like colonies – taking care not to shout this from the rooftops, however. 'All the necessary measures – firing squads, deportations, etc.' would be in force. As for the guerrilla war, it had its advantages: it would give us 'the opportunity to exterminate those who oppose us'. The occupied territories would have to be pacified: the most effective method would be 'for us to kill whoever even looks at us the wrong way'.[26]

On 22 July Hitler directed the commandants of the rear echelons to employ the harshest methods to impose order; all force must be brought to bear to keep the population under control.[27] The army high command in turn stated its position, three days later, in a reference to the partisans. The enemy taken in battle must be killed; in the event of passive resistance on the part of the civilian population, collective reprisals must be instituted; any 'suspicious elements', for whom an offence could not be proved but who seemed dangerous because of their opinions or attitude, must be turned over to the Einsatzgruppen.[28]

The murderous acts of the SS in the field reflected the mounting brutality that the course of the campaign, after only a few weeks, had aroused in the highest German officials. Nazi ideology had paved the way for this outburst of fury: the battle against an adversary both despised and demonized drove it to the most egregious excesses. The army itself, early on, had designated Jews as a category of suspicious and dangerous persons who must be treated with the utmost severity. The association between the Jews and the partisans was soon borne in on the military commanders of the rear echelons: the work of the SS would know no bounds.

On 22 July Hitler received a Croatian leader, Marshal Kvaternik. He told Kvaternik of his conviction that most of the enemy forces would be wiped out in six to eight weeks. He made a reference to history by declaring that Stalin, not he, would suffer Napoleon's fate: an illogical statement, but a psychologically revealing one. When the discussion moved on to Croatia's internal problems, Hitler urged his visitor to use the most brutal measures to achieve purification. 'Asocials' and criminals must be exterminated; when a country sends its best to risk their lives at the front, it need not spare the scum.

Returning to the situation in the east, he spoke again of the Jews, calling them 'the scourge of humanity'. They had exercised their power as Bolshevik commissars in the Baltic states; now, the inhabitants of those countries were wreaking a bloody vengeance on them. He expressed his wish to get them out of Europe: he was 'indifferent' as to whether they were sent to Madagascar or to Siberia.[29] Significantly, Hitler justified his obsessive desire for extermination by invoking the blood of soldiers killed in combat. But this obsession was only partly aimed at the Jews. While he spoke approvingly of the massacres taking place in the Baltic states, he attributed them to the natives and claimed no responsibility; he reaffirmed his intention to concentrate Europe's Jews in some sort of territory.

At the beginning of August, Hitler faced the same murky future. The initial schedule would not be met, and each day the risk grew that the campaign would not be over before winter. It was no longer a question of reaching Moscow on 15 August and ending the war on 1 October, as he had told Ambassador Schulenburg at the start of the campaign.[30] The disputes with his generals about operational tactics began again, with full force, resulting in unsatisfactory compromises that undermined morale. On 11 August Halder painted a grim picture of the situation in his journal. The 'Russian colossus' had been underestimated: instead of the 200 divisions anticipated, it produced 360; for every dozen divisions destroyed, another dozen replaced them, poorly equipped, but in position none the less. The enemy benefited, besides, from the proximity of its bases, while the German army moved ever further from its own. Finally, the enemy took advantage of the drawn-out German lines by raiding and harassing them.[31]

On 18 August the army proposed a plan of operations that gave priority to the capture of Moscow. Hitler flew into a rage and imposed his point of view in a style that brooked no further discussion. The enemy's vital economic centres – the region around Leningrad to the north, the Donetz basin and the Crimea to the south – must be taken before winter; an attack on Moscow would only be organized after the conclusion of these operations. From that time on, German leaders let it be known that they thought it less and less likely that the campaign would be over by winter. On 19 August the redeployment of the army, originally scheduled for the autumn, when Operation Barbarossa was to have ended, was postponed indefinitely. At the same time actions against England, planned in other theatres of operation, were abandoned.

The consequences of this unexpected prolongation of the campaign could not be ignored. In a memorandum written in the latter part of August, Keitel summarized the situation and spelled out the prospects. After eight weeks of fighting, despite dazzling successes, the Wehrmacht continued to run into Soviet resistance. If a sudden collapse of the enemy were possible, the probable course of events led in another direction. Keitel assumed as a working hypothesis that the enemy would not be entirely beaten by winter, and that operations would continue into the following year. He studied the consequences for the Reich's strategic position, all of which were negative. Japan would abandon the idea of an attack on Russia – which, as we know today, she would only have undertaken in the event of an immediate German victory. The joining of English and Soviet forces by way of Iran could not be prevented, for Turkey, like Spain and France, for that matter, would persist in its neutrality. The Axis position in the Mediterranean would grow more problematic. And finally, while an Anglo-American invasion of Europe was not to be feared for the near future, the situation could change drastically if North Africa fell into enemy hands: in that event, Italy would be directly threatened.

The Reich's ultimate goal, Keitel stressed, remained the defeat of Great Britain. But it was a goal that had become more difficult than ever to achieve. Keitel's report shows that American intervention was thought to be inevitable; it was only a matter of time. The signing of the Altantic Charter by Churchill and Roosevelt on 11 August had dramatically demonstrated the solidarity of the two Anglo-Saxon countries. So even if the enemy to the east were beaten the following spring, the fighting would still be far from over. Soviet resistance pointed to an indefinite prolongation of the war, the shift from a lightning war to an extended war. All these points can be read between the lines of Keitel's memorandum; it is unlikely that Hitler was not aware of them, even though he did not choose to admit it. In any case, he approved the document and authorized that it be sent to the commanders of his three armed services as well as to von Ribbentrop; but he forbade its reproduction or distribution to anyone else.[32]

In fact, Hitler had probably began early in August to foresee a prolongation of the war. Each time he received foreign visitors, usually from allied countries, he asserted emphatically that the worst was over and victory was at hand. However, doubts and reservations regularly penetrated this façade of optimism. Meeting with Antonescu on 6 August, he twice used the word 'hope' in relation to the goals he had set himself: he 'hoped' to seize the enemy's leading economic centres; he 'hoped' to achieve these objectives before the bad weather set in.[33] Compared with the original objective, the Volga – Archangel line, the scaling down of ambitions was important. Hitler also knew that Stalin had major industrial centres at his disposal behind the Urals, and that each week that went by gave him time to move his factories and workers to the rear. He preferred to minimize their importance, probably not convincing himself, and to stifle his growing certainty that the war was bogging down.

On 25 August he met with Mussolini and gave his customary victory speech. The enemy would collapse in October at the latest, under repeated assaults; the loss of its economic bases would complete the rout. During the same conversation, however, he said that it mattered little whether the collapse occurred in the near future, in a few months, or even the following spring: the instruments of victory, he assured Mussolini, were in Germany's hands.[34] An Italian diplomat who attended this meeting wrote that the German leaders showed an 'optimism in principle' but that they still had not recovered from the shock of the Soviet resistance.[35]

The most obvious signs of Hitler's disarray were the hopes for peace that he began to entertain. On 18 August he raised with an amazed Goebbels the possibility of a peace offer from Stalin. He said he would be willing to accept, on the condition that he received extensive territorial guarantees and the disarmament of the enemy down to the last gun; the Bolshevik regime could then expand as it pleased on the far side of the Urals. Obviously, the demands he mentioned could only be imposed on the heels of a crushing victory. But if he was ready to make peace with Stalin, Hitler must no longer have felt so confident about utterly annihilating him. During the same conversation with Goebbels, he also remarked that peace might come suddenly: perhaps Churchill would fall?[36] In the following weeks, he spoke on several occasions of the possibility of a sudden end to the war with the Soviet Union. Stalin might be overthrown or, again, might show that he was disposed to conclude an armistice or a peace. He, Hitler, would concur if Stalin agreed to retreat into Asia, or, better still, if he agreed to expand toward the Persian Gulf, which would put him in conflict with Great Britain and further the Reich's causes.[37] Hitler dreamed of a miraculous peace which would rescue him from the trap he saw closing around him.

Concurrently, his attitude toward the Jews hardened. Around 8 or 10 August, during one of the monologues he habitually delivered late into the night, which Bormann had recently decided to note down, he spoke of population evacuations. If any country had the right to effect one, it was Germany: was it not true that several hundred thousand Germans had been forced to leave East Prussia after the Great War? He did not understand how anyone could see an act of extreme brutality in the evacuation of 600,000 Jews.[38] He reiterated to Goebbels his desire to expel the Jews from the Reich during the 18 August conversation, in which he decided to make them wear an insignia. Referring to their deportation to the east after the war, he added that the harsh climate would teach them how to live.

Most importantly, however, he made reference to his 'prophecy'. 'During these past weeks and months', he said, it was coming true with an almost terrifying certainty. 'In the east, the Jews are being forced to foot the bill for the damage; in Germany they have already paid in part and will have to pay even more in the future.'[39] Here the massacre of the Russian Jews was identified and laid claim to; it was referred to as a recent occurrence, linked to the turn the war had taken. The Jews had to 'foot the bill'; indeed, vengeance was being wreaked on them because of spilled German blood. Hitler was also determined to wreak his vengeance on the German Jews, with a force that remained undecided: their fate could be as cruel as the one inflicted on the Soviet Jews, or it could be more lenient. The idea of extermination was taking shape in proportion to the difficulties encountered in the war in the east; but the final verdict clearly had not been reached.

It is significant that, in his monologues that summer and autumn, Hitler brooded about the memory of 1918. The situation in which he found himself invited comparison with the traumatizing experience that had shaped his political universe. Four hundred more tanks in the summer of 1918, and Germany would have won the war! More troops on the right flank in 1918, and victory would have been theirs![40] Many such remarks revealed that he felt himself to be walking a tightrope. And the comparison was not limited to the military plane. During the evening of 14 September he raised the subject of the 1918 revolution and its leaders who had emerged, according to him, from prison lowlife. There was something that would not happen again: he had ordered Himmler, in the event of internal troubles, to kill all concentration camp prisoners; thus no leader would appear to incite masses.[41]

The situation was not so bad, on the other hand, that he sank into despair. During those same weeks of September and October, when preparations for the genocide were beginning, we see him also exuding hope and confidence – although the limits and source of such feelings must be acknowledged. He had been forced to admit that, in all probability, the war would not be over by the onset of winter; but he wanted all the more desperately to believe in a reversal of the situation that at a stroke would make up for the delay. In September the offensive in the south was crowned with success with the capture of Kiev, the Donetz basin, and part of the Crimea. Hitler then decided to launch an offensive aimed at Moscow, which paid off in mid-October with the double victory of Briansk and Viazma. The enemy had suffered considerable losses; but once again it had succeeded in keeping a large part of its army from being surrounded.

On the eve of this offensive, Hitler had it trumpeted in the press that victory was now certain. He was certainly motivated by tactics of psychological warfare, as well as by the wish to rebuild confidence in his allies and the German people. But his behaviour also reflected an ardent belief in a decisive victory, a belief which only partially masked an ineradicable anxiety. In the speech he made to the soldiers on the eastern front on 2 October, he emphasized that all necessary preparations had been made to defeat the enemy, but he thought it wise to specify 'in so far as men can be the masters'. In an address the following day, in which he also proclaimed victory, he casually mentioned a hypothetical prolongation of the war.[42] His hopes, like his bursts of confidence, in reality were the euphoric other side of a fundamentally dark and tormented frame of mind.[43] If he had really been convinced at the time that a final victory in the east was at hand, he would not have ordered the immediate deportation of the Jews, the opposite of his earlier policy.

During the same period, in fact, in his messages and speeches, he denounced the Jews with increasing violence as the sole perpetrators of the war, as adversaries who, under the double cover of capitalism and Bolshevism, had sworn to annihilate national socialism and to exterminate the German people.[44] On 3 October he attacked all those who had pushed

Churchill into the war and had rejoiced to see it erupt on 1 September 1939, adding: 'perhaps from now on they will see this ravishing war in a different light.'[45] The Jews were not explicitly mentioned, but they were unmistakably alluded to; in so far as Hitler was referring (as I believe he was) to an exterminatory vengeance, the 'from now on' leads us to conclude that a decision had recently been made.

In private, he would be more open in the following weeks, without entirely abandoning his allusive language. His September monologues reveal nothing significant; those from the end of October, on the other hand, are eloquent. On 23 October he said, in talking about the Jews, that 'by exterminating this plague' he would strike a blow for humanity that the German people could not yet comprehend.[46] On 25 October, in the presence of Himmler and Heydrich, he recalled his prophecy, adding that the Jews already had the two million Germans killed in the First World War on their conscience and now some hundred thousand more. 'No one had better say: "but we still can't drive them into the swamp!" Does no one care about our men? It is a good thing we are preceded by the ominous reputation of exterminating the Jews. The attempt to found a Jewish state will be a failure.'[47]

Here again, the link between spilled German blood and the death of the Jews is clearly established. The penultimate sentence remains partly obscure, although not without interest. It points up Hitler's ambiguous attitude toward his act of extermination. On the one hand, he was anxious to keep it secret; as he said on 21 October, the German people were not yet in a position to understand the service he was rendering humanity. On the other hand, he felt compelled to declare and claim it. After the end of the year he would repeat his prophecy on several public occasions, making it clear that it was on the road to fulfilment. He wanted the Jewish adversary to know what it would cost to oppose him.

The progress of the campaign in the last two months of the year confirmed his worst fears. In November he tried to force the issue by launching a new offensive on Moscow, despite the weather conditions, the lack of winter equipment, and the state of his supplies. Frantically seeking a victory, he fought for objectives that betrayed the precariousness of his position; the offensive was meant primarily to weaken the enemy so that preparations for springtime operations could proceed

safely. It had no more success than the first one. Now it was
the enemy who was on the offensive, bringing the advance
of the German army to an abrupt halt and coming within an
inch of inflicting a disaster on it.

Operation Barbarossa had failed decisively. The Nazi generals finally had to admit what they had not wanted to
acknowledge at the end of October. And yet, at that point,
there had been no doubt that the gamble was lost, from a
military point of view as well as from an economic one. The
war had cost the German army so much, in men and material,
that its fighting force was now crippled; Halder noted on 23
November that in future the Reich would never have at its
disposal an army such as the one it boasted on 22 June 1941.[48]
The Russian campaign had also thrown the German economy
into a serious crisis; shortages of manpower and raw materials were so critical that the production of armaments was
threatened. On 29 November the Minister of Armaments
and Munitions, Todt, told Hitler that the war could only
be concluded favourably for the Reich through negotiations;
militarily and economically, it had already been lost.[49]

A week earlier, Hitler had found himself alone with
Goebbels, who asked him point-blank if he believed in a
victory. He answered that if he had had faith in a victory
in 1918 when he was only a corporal, half-blinded and lying
in a hospital bed, how much more would he believe in it
now that he was in command of the most powerful army
in the world and dominated almost all of Europe.[50] He was,
in a way, admitting that the road to victory would be long
and hard, and that it would require the same astonishing
succession of favourable conditions as in the past. In early
December the Japanese attack on Pearl Harbor prompted
him to declare war on the United States, thus reassuring his
ally and expressing his willingness to fight an enemy whose
intervention he considered inevitable. Now he found himself
in the same position as the former imperial Germany, the
position he had always wished to avoid.

Hitler had not waited for the United States' entry into
the war before activating the extermination machinery. The
decision had arisen from a murderous rage increasingly exac-
erbated by the ordeal of the failure of his campaign in Russia
and, through it, the failure of his entire venture. By August
he knew that a definitive victory in the east before winter was
hardly likely, that the war would extend into the next year.

As a result, British resistance would be galvanized, and an American intervention made all the more probable. Perhaps he underestimated the obstacles that still might delay that intervention; but all that mattered now was the feeling he had of an ineluctable event. Under these conditions, there was no need to wait for the war to become officially a world war.

Since his entry into politics, Hitler had pondered the possibility of failure and had marshalled his responses. He knew the danger, and recognized it when it arose: the war dragging on with, at its end, the spectre of defeat. Around the middle of September 1941, when he decided to kill the Jews, he certainly did not think defeat was inevitable. But he must have felt that it would take a great deal of luck in the future for him to win; and he saw clearly the price he would have to pay to avoid defeat. The extermination of the Jews, then, was at once a propitiatory act and an act of vengeance. By putting to death those he thought of as his archetypal enemies – little did it matter to his obsessed mind that these were powerless civilian populations – he was demonstrating his will to fight to the end. By means of the somehow sacrificial death of the Jews, he was fanatically steeling himself to achieve victory, or fight on to destruction. At the same time, and above all, he was expiating spilled German blood, and avenging beforehand a possible defeat. He would conduct this exercise of vengeance, as it turned out, with mounting determination as the situation worsened, and he advanced toward an apocalyptic end.

7

Conclusion

For a half a century, the Final Solution has weighed on the European conscience. Whether it is a matter of denying it, or evaluating its singularity, it continues to engage minds and wrench hearts.[1] It also continues to hold the attention of the historian, confronted with the double task of reconstructing the event in its multiple dimensions and of comprehending its nature. The techniques of the profession suffice for the first of these tasks although, with the sorry state of our source material, the various reconstructions can only aspire to a greater or lesser degree of coherence and credibility. For the second task, however, the resources of reflection seem hopelessly limited: the event, in its enormity and diversity, remains largely unfathomable. As Saul Friedländer wrote, 'the paralysis of the historian derives from the simultaneity and interaction of entirely heterogeneous phenomena: messianic fanaticism and bureaucratic structures, pathological impulses and administrative decrees, archaic attitudes and an advanced industrial society'.[2]

The slaughter of European Jews was an enterprise to which countless people throughout Europe contributed. From zeal to complicity, from acquiescence to passivity, everything served its accomplishment. The machinery, once activated, functioned as if by inertia: the crime was, to a large extent, a crime of bureaucrats. Each person accomplished his task by concentrating on the link in the chain that concerned him, a chain whose end was death itself. But while the actual work of the Final Solution, directly and indirectly, was an anonymous business, cold and compartmentalized, one man, animated by intense convictions, played a pivotal role in bringing it to pass and sustaining its momentum. In matters of extermination, Hitler had the last word; he was the prime mover.

In May of 1942, Greiser wrote to Himmler informing him

that the extermination of the Jews in the Wartheland was nearing completion; he now wished to inflict the same fate on some 30,000 Poles suffering from tuberculosis. Himmler adjutantly replied on 14 May that his proposal had been submitted to Heydrich for his opinion, but that the final decision could only be made by the Führer.[3] It would be astonishing if it had been otherwise for the fate of millions of Jews.

If Hitler had died in the summer of 1941, would the final solution have taken place? Without him, the decisive thrust would probably have been absent. The Jews would have suffered in a Europe controlled by Goering, Goebbels, or Himmler. The segregation policy would have been pursued, atrocities would have occurred, perhaps mass violence. But for things to escalate into a holocaust Hitler's impetus was needed, an impetus with deep roots. Hitler did not stumble onto extermination by accident, neither did he opt for it in desperation when other solutions had failed. Nor did he exterminate the Jews merely to implement a programme he had sworn to carry out regardless of the circumstances.

His anti-Semitism had provided him with both orientations and resolutions, the sum of which added up to less than a master plan but more than a simple obsession. These elements were enough to inspire and guide his actions, even though they were somewhat vague, and produced dilemmas and conflicting priorities. Since the end of the 1930s, in any case, two lines of thought had coexisted in his mind and determined his attitude: the search for a territorial solution in case of victory, and a drastic revenge should the tide turn against him. Between these two policies, which both aimed at liberating Europe from its Jews, there was no definite, clear-cut opposition; the one was an extension of the other. Concentration in a reservation would have entailed a drastic reduction of the Jewish population. In this, however, the Jews would have shared the fate of the Slavic populations of eastern Europe, whose deportation to Siberia would have cost millions of lives. Extermination was another method of effecting the disappearance of the Jews from Europe. But here, between the one and the other, a threshold existed: to cross it, Hitler would have to be faced with a situation he had always dreaded. He would also have to have the feeling that the enterprise was feasible.

In the summer of 1940, at the peak of his success, he was

prepared to send Europe's Jews overseas. While he was gearing up for the Russian campaign, confident of victory, he made no moves against them. Then the campaign took an unexpected downturn whose mounting danger he perceived with an acuity born of long mental preparation: he was, properly speaking, the master of that situation. Far from showing a radicalization, his attitude was one of frightening fixity: the attitude of a man who has long contemplated his fall and decided on his responses to it.

But even if Hitler's mind had long been made up, and even if he had no need to radicalize his resolve, he had to actualize it, to decide at which point the time had come to act. The Soviet Jews were the victims of the rage that mounted in him as he felt his way, bolstered by the murderous frisson he sensed running through many parts of his regime. At a certain moment, very probably in September, he made the leap: the familiar storm clouds of another long war had engulfed his mind. By this decision, he regained the initiative he felt he was losing on the battlefield. Confronted by the probable failure of his plan for world domination, he burned his bridges by deciding to destroy those responsible for his downfall; he would persevere in the military conflict and in the massacre of the innocents until he had reduced Germany to ruins.

Early in the autumn of 1941, the spectre of a long war had persuaded him to take the plunge; the advent of total war allowed his decision to take effect. At all levels of government, men who, on their own, under other circumstances, would never have participated in or tolerated such an undertaking, carried it out with zeal, or at least allowed it to go forward. The army had paved the way: faced with the unyielding resistance of the Soviet enemy, it had reacted with a violence that fostered the frenzy of killing. In the rear, the ordeals suffered by the civilian population deadened normal sensibilities, while the regime tightened its grip. Churches which had protested against 'Operation Euthanasia' fell silent at the deportation of the Jews.

By dragging on, the war not only hardened the ideological principles, above all the anti-communism, which the German elite shared with the core of the regime; it also buttressed the widespread moral indifference which perhaps was the most effective facilitator of the Final Solution. It also radicalized an ideological streak in hard-core Nazis which Hitler knew exactly how to cultivate, and which served to steel their wills and justify their actions. Germans were going to spill their blood in the war; the Jews, however, threatened to survive it and emerge its victors. This image, as we have seen, was at the heart of Hitler's nightmare; it spurred him to revenge. Thus he said in a speech delivered in Berlin on 30 January 1942, right after alluding to his prophecy: 'For the first time, other people will not be the only ones to spill their blood; this time, for the first time, the old Jewish law will be in effect: an eye for an eye, and a tooth for a tooth.'[4]

Here once again, Hitler was the master of the situation. He encouraged, and fired up to an exterminatory fervour, the murderous reservoir of hatred in his fellow party members; a hatred which, left to itself, would probably not have escalated into genocide. On 18 August 1941, Goebbels fumed that the Germans not only had to wage war, but also had to feed the Jews 'who only want our defeat'. On 26 August he noted that, as long as Germany was fighting for her life, he would make sure the Jews neither profited from the war nor were spared by it.[5] When Frank informed his associates on 16 December 1941 of the decision to kill the Jews, he declared that, as an 'old national-Socialist', he had the following to say: if the Jews survived the war while Germans sacrificed their 'best blood', then the war would only be a partial success.[6] Here Frank visualized a German final victory; how much more urgent a massacre would seem if the prospect were defeat. Several ranks below, Eichmann's assistant, Frank Novak, testified during his trial that the justification for the murder of the Jews had been the fact that countless Germans would die in the war, while the Jews would emerge unscathed.[7]

This representation evolved directly from the experience of 1918, from the stereotypes and attitudes that the trauma of defeat had embedded in the German far right. A race of cowards, the Jews did not make war; a race of profiteers, they pushed others to kill one another in order to consolidate their own power; a satanic race, they had formed a world conspiracy against Germany and vowed the extermination of the German people. The destructive force of this vision was redoubled by the Nazis' biologism, which caused them to ascribe such importance to German blood, its preservation, and its increase. The ancient response of blood crying out for vengeance found a modern outlet in their racist ideology.

Extermination struck down the Jews because they were the incarnation of everything despicable and menacing: liberalism and democracy, materialism and hedonism, and especially Marxism, which provoked the most virulent reactions. For all that, it is incorrect to make anti-Bolshevism, rather than anti-Semitism, the motivating force behind the Final Solution.[8] The Nazis' hatred of communism, and the identification they made between it and Judaism, certainly explain the brutality of their actions during the first weeks of the Russian campaign, as well as the escalation of that brutality when the fighting took an unexpected turn. But the prolongation of the war in the east did not, by itself, bring on the extermination of the European Jews. The American factor was just as decisive: the adversities encountered in the east reinforced the probability of United States intervention in the war, and of the eventual defeat of the Reich.

In the summer of 1941, with a rapprochement taking place between the Soviet Union and the Anglo-Saxon countries, Hitler found himself facing a global coalition, an alliance he immediately blamed on the machinations of the Jews. The extermination of those within his reach was therefore much more than the product of his anti-Bolshevism. It was the monstrous fruit of his hatred of a world enemy, which had assumed the opposing faces of capitalism and Bolshevism and was now removing its masks to reveal itself in its diabolical unity. The European Jews thus met a fate that was inexorable. Europe could only have been rescued from the Nazi yoke by Soviet resistance and American intervention; but with the globalization of the conflict, the death penalty was pronounced on her Jews. The liberation of Europe was paid for with Jewish lives.

Notes

Abbreviations

ADAP	*Akten zur deutschen auswärtigen Politik*
BAK	Bundesarchiv Koblenz
BA-MA	Bundesarchiv-Militärarchiv (Freiburg i.B.)
CDJC	Centre de documentation juive contemporaine (Paris)
IHTP	Institut d'histoire du temps présent (Paris)
PA-AA	Politisches Archiv des Auswärtigen Amtes (Bonn)
TMI	*International Military Tribunal: Trial of the Major War Criminals* (42 vols., Nuremberg, 1949)
VfZ	*Vierteljahreshefte für Zeitgeschichte*
ZStL	Zentrale Stelle der Landesjustizverwaltungen (Ludwigsburg)

Introduction to the English Edition

1. Karl A. Schleunes, *The Twisted Road to Auschwitz: The Nazi Policy Towards German Jews, 1933–1939* (Urbana: Univ. of Illinois Press, 1970).
2. Helmut Krausnick and Hans-Heinrich Wilhelm, *Die Truppe des Weltanschauungskrieges: Die Einsatzgruppen der Sicherheitspolizei und des SD, 1938–1942* (Stuttgart: Deutsche Verlagsanstalt, 1982); Helmut Krausnick, 'Hitler und die Befehle an die Einsatzgruppen im Sommer 1941', in Eberhard Jäckel and Jürgen Rohwer (eds.), *Der Mord an den Juden im Zweiten Weltkrieg* (Stuttgart: Deutsche Verlagsanstalt, 1985).
3. *Sowjetische Gefangene in Hitlers Vernichtungskrieg: Berichte und Dokumente, 1941–1945* (Heidelberg: C. F. Miller, 1982); 'Zur Eröffnung des allgemeinen Judenvernichtungsbefehls gegenüber den Einsatzgruppen', in Jäckel and Rohwer, *op. cit.* The general line of Streim's argument was followed by Arno Mayer in his history of the 'Final Solution', *Why Did the Heavens Not Darken? The 'Final Solution' in History* (New York: Pantheon, 1988).
4. This conclusion is confirmed not only by Alfred Streim's research but

by the findings of Israeli scholars as well. See esp. Yaacov Lozowick, 'Rollbahn Mord: The Early Activities of Einsatzgruppe C', *Holocaust and Genocide Studies*, 2/2 (1987), 221 ff.

5. See e.g. his reference to the research of Yehoshua Buechler, 'Kommandostab Reichsfuehrer SS: Himmler's Personal Murder Brigades in 1941', *Holocaust and Genocide Studies*, 1(1) (1986).

6. Christopher Browning, *Ordinary Men* New York: Harper, (1992).

7. *Vilna Hayehudit Bemaavak Uvechilayon* Tel Aviv: Sifriat Poalim, 1976, 72. If one takes vol. ii of the history of Lithuanian Jewry, dealing with the period of the Holocaust, the first page, listing alphabetically the entries indicating the extermination sites and dates of the Lithuanian communities, gives the following dates (day, month, year): 25.8.41; 29.8.41; 30.7.41; 2.10.41; 8.12.41; 31.7.41; 7.8.41; 29.8.41; 29.8.41; 9.8.41; 12.8.41; 17.8.41; 9.9.41; 29.8.41; 26.8.41; 3.9.41; 29.8.41; 23.6.41; 13–31.8.41; 9.9.41; June 41; 14.8.41; 30.8.41; 24.12.41. *Yahadut Lita: Hashoah 1941–1945* Tel Aviv, 1984, 481. These dates confirm the thesis of an incremental process.

8. Arad, *op. cit.*, 73.

9. *The Architect of Genocide: Himmler and the Final Solution* (New York: Knopf, 1991), 169–70.

10. *Fateful Months: Essays on the Emergence of the 'Final Solution'* (New York: Holmes & Meier, 1985); Raul Hilberg, *The Destruction of the European Jews* rev. edn. (3 vols., New York: Holmes & Meier, 1985); Krausnick, *op. cit.*

11. *Fateful Months*, 8.

12. Uwe Dietrich Adam, *Judenpolitik im Dritten Reich* (Düsseldorf: Droste, 1972); Eberhard Jäckel, *Hitlers Herrschaft: Vollzug einer Weltanschauung* (Stuttgart: Deutsche Verlagsanstalt, 1986).

13. See esp. Martin Broszat, 'Hitler und die Genesis der "Endlösung": Auf Anlass der Thesen von David Irving', *VfZ* 25/4 (Oct. 1977) (English trans: *Yad Vashem Studies*, 13 (1979); Hans Mommsen, 'The Realisation of the Unthinkable: The "Final Solution" of the Jewish Question in the Third Reich', in Gerhard Hirschfeld (ed.), *The Policies of Genocide: Jews and Soviet Prisoners of War in Nazi Germany*, London: Allen & Unwin, 1986; Mayer, *op. cit.*

14. Saul Friedländer, 'From Antisemitism to Extermination: A Historiographical Study of Nazi Policies Towards the Jews', *Yad Vashem Studies*, 16 (1984).

15. On this controversy, see Charles S. Maier, *The Unmasterable Past* (Cambridge, Mass.: Harvard Univ. Press, 1988); Richard J. Evans, *In Hitler's Shadow: West German Historians and the Attempt to Escape from the Nazi Past* New York: Pantheon, 1989; Peter Baldwin (ed.), *Reworking the Past: Hitler, the Holocaust and the Historians' Debate* (Boston: Beacon, 1990).

16. Ulrich Herbert, 'Arbeit und Vernichtung: Ökonomisches Interesse und Primat der "Weltanschauung" im Nationalsozialismus', in Dan Diner (ed.), *Ist der Nationalsozialismus Geschichte? Zu Historisierung und Historikerstreit* (Frankfurt: Fischer, 1988), 213, 234.

Introduction

1. Raul Hilberg's book, *La Destruction des Juifs d'Europe* (Paris, Fayard,

1988; 1st edn. 1961) is the reference work. I will, however, make the following reservation. Hilberg is above all interested in the manner in which the genocide was carried out. He offers a model: in order that the Jews may be killed, they must first be identified, dispossessed, concentrated, and transported. This is logically true, but the problem is that he presents events as if historical development had actually followed this logical pattern. Whence the driving force attributed to some unknown bureaucratic determinism which, once launched on its work of persecution, could only have ended in extermination. Whence also the reference in only a few pages, at the beginning of the chapter on the deportations (338 ff.), to the Nazi emigration policy and the plans for a Jewish reservation as if they were only short-term deviations, of no serious consequence to the course that led to the Holocaust.

2. Let us cite as examples Karl Dietrich Bracher, *La Dictature allemande* (Toulouse, Privat, 1986); Eberhard Jäckel, *Hitler idéologue* (Paris, Calmann-Lévy, 1973); Lucy S. Dawidowicz, *The War Against the Jews* (New York, Holt, 1975); Gerald Fleming, *Hitler und die Endlösung* (Wiesbaden and Munich, Limes, 1982); Helmut Krausnick, 'Judenverfolgung', in *Anatomie des SS-Staates*, ii (Munich, Deutscher Taschenbuch Verlag, 1967).

3. Among these historians, who follow in the footsteps of Ernst Fraenkel (*The Dual State*, Oxford Univ. Press, 1941) and Franz Neumann (*Béhémoth*, Paris, Payot, 1987; 1st English edn. 1944), let us cite Martin Broszat, *L'État hitlérien* (Paris, Fayard, 1985); Karl A. Schleunes, *The Twisted Road to Auschwitz: Nazi Policy Toward the German Jews* (Urbana, Univ. of Illinois Press, 1970); Uwe Dietrich Adam, *Judenpolitik im Dritten Reich* (Düsseldorf, Droste, 1972). We also find in Joseph Billig, *La Solution finale de la question juive* (Paris, Klarsfeld, 1977), 47 ff., a point of view that stresses Hitler's indecision and the pioneering role of his lieutenants in the Holocaust. Léon Poliakov, *Bréviaire de la haine* (Paris, Calmann-Lévy, 1951) also maintains that Hitler did not intend to exterminate the Jews: the Nazis arrived at the Holocaust 'in spite of themselves and, in a way, pushed, swept along by the demons they had unleashed' 3–4).

4. The title of a work published in 1946, Walter Petwaidic, *Die autoritäre Anarchie* (Hamburg).

5. Cf. Martin Broszat, 'Hitler und die Genesis der "Endlösung" ', *VfZ* 4 (1977), 739–75; Hans Mommsen, 'Die Realisierung des Utopischen: Die"Endlösung der Judenfrage" im "Dritten Reich" ', *Geschichte und Gesellschaft*, 3 (1983), 381–420.

6. For the debate between these two trends, see the symposia *L'Allemagne nazie et le Génocide juif* (Paris, Gallimard–Le Seuil, 1985); *Der Mord an den Juden im Zweiten Weltkrieg*, ed. E. Jäckel and J. Rohwer (Stuttgart, Denutsche Verlags-Anstalt 1985), as well as the Paris symposium of Dec. 1987, *La Politique nazie d'extermination* (Paris, Albin Michel, 1989). See also Michael R. Marrus, *Holocaust in History* (London, Univ. Press of New England, 1987) and, more generally, Ian Kershaw, *The Nazi Dictatorship: Problems and Perspectives of Interpretation*, 2nd edn. (London, Edward Arnold, 1989).

7. Saul Friedländer stressed this central role of Hitler's, notably in a seminal article, 'From Antisemitism to Extermination', *Yad Vashem Studies*, 16 (1984), 1–50.
8. Cf. Eberhard Jäckel, *Hitler in History* (Hanover and London, Univ. Press of New England, 1984), 44–65, and *Hitlers Herrschaft* (Stuttgart, Deutsche Verlags-Anstalt, 1986), 89–122. Cf. also S. Haffner, *Un certain Adolf Hitler* (Paris, Grasset, 1979), 217–18.
9. Among Christopher Browning's works, see esp. *Fateful Months: Essays on the Emergence of the Final Solution* (New York, Holmes & Meier, 1985).
10. Arno Mayer, *Why Did the Heavens Not Darken? The Final Solution in History* (New York, Pantheon, 1989).

1. Hitler's Anti-Semitism

1. Detlef Grieswelle, 'Hitlers Rhetorik in der Weimarer Zeit' (diss., Univ. of Saarbrück, 1969), 356–8.
2. See Hermann Rauschning, *Hitler Told Me* (Paris, Coopération, 1939), 57–9, 159–60. Like many other historians, I estimate that Rauschning's evidence is admissible in its general outline. On the political and social aspects of Hitlerian idéology, see Rainer Zitelmann, *Hitler: Selbstverständnis eines Revolutionärs* (Hamburg, Berg, 1987).
3. *Sämtliche Aufzeichnungen, 1905–1924*, ed. E. Jäckel and A. Kuhn (Stuttgart, Deutsche Verlags-Anstalt, 1980), no. 578, p. 1025–6.
4. *Mein Kampf* (Paris, Nouvelles editions latines, n.d. (1934)), 254, 402.
5. Ibid. 250 ff., 402–4.
6. Ibid. 689.
7. Ibid. 225. For the influence of the Great War on Hitler, see Rudolph Binion, *Hitler Among the Germans* (New York, Elsevier, 1976); see also his enriching article, 'Der Jude ist weg: Machtpolitische Auswirkungen des hitlerschen Rassengedankens', in *Die deutsche Frage im 19 und 20. Jahrhundert*, ed. J. Becker and A. Hillgruber (Munich, Vögel, 1983), 347–72.
8. *Sämtliche Aufzeichnungen*, no. 566, p. 1003; *Mein Kampf*, 169–70, 517–18, 677.
9. Ibid. 680.
10. Ibid. 71.
11. Ibid. 205
12. Ibid. 653.
13. *Sämtliche Aufzeichnungen*, no. 103, p. 138; no. 109, p. 148; no. 113, p. 153.
14. Ibid. no. 388, p. 644. These aspects have already been brought out by Jäckel, *Hitler idéologue*, 71.
15. *Mein Kampf*, 660.
16. Cf. e.g. *Sämtliche Aufzeichnungen*, no. 173, p. 276; *Mein Kampf*, 324.
17. Victor Klemperer, *Lingua Tertii Imperii* (Leipzig, Reclam, 1966; 1st edn. 1946), 71.

18. 'Sein letztes Ziel aber muss unverrückbar die Entfernung der Juden überhaupt sein', *Sämtliche Aufzeichnungen*, no. 61, pp. 89–90.
19. e.g. ibid. no. 91, p. 120, no. 98, p. 128.
20. '. . . absolut nur als Gäste', BAK, NS26/55, speech of 7 Dec. 1928, p. 33.
21. This is what he claimed on 18 Sept. 1922 (*Sämtliche Aufzeichnungem*, no. 405, p. 690).
22. Rauschning, *Hitler Told Me*, 264.
23. *Sämtliche Aufzeichnungen*, no. 421, p. 727 (13 Nov. 1922).
24. *Hitler: Memoirs of a Confidant*, ed. H. A. Turner, Jr. (New Haven and London, Yale Univ. Press, 1985), p. 186.
25. William Carr, *Hitler: A Study in Personality and Politics* (London, Edward Arnold, 1978), 177, n. 25.
26. *Mein Kampf*, 649.
27. We have a perfect example in a speech delivered by Hitler on 29 Apr. 1937; see *Es spricht der Führer: Sieben exemplarische Hitler-Reden*, ed. H. von Kotze and H. Krausnick (Gütersloh, Mohn, 1966), 147–8.
28. See Stephen Wilson, *Ideology and Experience: Anti-Semitism in France at the Time of the Dreyfus Affair* (London, Associated Univ. Press, 1982).
29. This criticism could be directed at Jäckel's work, *Hitler idéologue*.
30. *Mein Kampf*, 170.
31. Ibid. 677–8.
32. *Hitler sans masque: Entretiens Hitler – Breiting* ed. E. Calic (Paris, Stock, 1969), 82. On this work and its editor, see *Reichstagsbrand: Aufklärung einer historischen Legende*, ed. U. Backes *et al.* (Munich, Piper, 1986).
33. For the last quotation, see *Le Troisième Reich et les Juifs*, Comité pour la défense des droits des Juifs Anvers, 1933), 94. For the other examples see *Die Stellung der NSDAP zur Judenfrage*, ed. Centralverein deutscher Staatsbürger jüdischen Glaubens (Berlin, n.d.), unpaginated.
34. Passage from an Oct. 1935 article in *Judenkenner* (Berlin), quoted by Hans-Günther Adler, *Der verwaltete Mensch* (Tübingen, Mohr, 1974), 60. See also Herbert A. Strauss, 'Hostages of"World Jewry": On the Origins of the Idea of Genocide in German History', *Holocaust and Genocide Studies*, (1988), 125–36.

2. The Emigration Policy, 1933–1939

1. Adam, *Judenpolitik*, 28–33.
2. '[Hitler] ist nun zum Entschluss gekommen', in *Die Tagebücher von Joseph Goebbels*, ed. E. Fröhlich (Munich, K. G. Saus, 1987), 1/2, p. 398.
3. Helmut Genschel, *Die Verdrängung der Juden aus der Wirtschaft im Dritten Reich* (Göttingen, Musterschmidt, 1966), 56.
4. *Akten der Reichskanzlei Regierung Hitler 1933–1938* (Boppard a.R., Harald Boldt, 1983), p. i, doc. 193, p. 677.
5. Genschel, *Verdrängung*, 47.

6. Eliahu Ben Elissar, *La Diplomatie du IIIe Reich et les Juifs, 1933–1939* (Paris, Julliard, 1968), 38.
7. *Akten der Reichskanzlei*, doc. 193, p. 675.
8. Ibid. doc. 180, pp. 631–3.
9. Genschel, *Verdrängung*, 81–2.
10. See Gisela Bock, *Zwangssterilisation im National-sozialismus* (Opladen, Westdeutscher Verlag, 1986).
11. Ben Elissar, *Diplomatie*, 150–5.
12. Schleunes, *Twisted Road* 178–80.
13. Ben Elissar, *Diplomatie*, 85 ff.
14. Genschel, *Verdrängung*, 109.
15. 'Er ist sehr zugünglich. In vielem wird es nun bald Änderung geben', in *Tagebücher von Joseph Goebbels*, I/2, p. 488.
16. Genschel, *Verdrängung*, 114. On the chaotic conditions surrounding the birth of these laws, see Lothar Gruchmann, 'Blutschutzgesetz und Justiz: Zur Entstehung und Wirkung des Nürnberger Gesetzes vom 15. September 1935' *VjZ* (July 1983), 418–42.
17. 'Bericht des mit der Führung der Geschäfte beauftragten SS-Sturmmann Dr. Schlösser über die Besprechung im Rassenpolitischen Amt vom 25.9.1935', BAK, NS2/143.
18. 'Das Reichministerium des Innern und die Judengesetzgebung', *VjZ* (July 1961), 281.
19. Adam, *Judenpolitik*, 135 ff.
20. *Tagebücher von Joseph Goebbels*, T/2, pp. 520, 537, 540.
21. Schleunes's view that Hitler played a 'hesitant and indecisive' role during these years seems excessive to me (*Twisted Road*, 131.)
22. e.g. *Tagebücher von Joesph Goebbels*, I/2, 19 Aug. 1935, p. 504; 29 May 1936, p. 618; 15 Nov. 1936, p. 727.
23. Ibid. 23 Feb. 1937, I/3, p. 55.
24. Ibid. I/3, p. 351.
25. BAK, R18/5514, 'Vermerk über die Besprechung am 29 September, 1936'.
26. Adam, *Judenpolitik*, 200; Ben Elissar, *Diplomatie*, 216, 219 ff.
27. Ibid. 183–4.
28. Adam, *Judenpolitik*, 161–2; Genschel, *Verdrängung*, 142 n. 9.
29. Hubert Rosenkranz, *Verfolgung und Selbstbehauptung: Die Juden in Osterreich 1938–1945* (Vienna, Harold, 1978), 27.
30. Genschel, *Verdrängung*, 150.
31. Rosenkranz, *Verfolgung*, 106.
32. Genschel, *Verdrängung*, 150.
33. Ibid. 168–72.
34. *Tagebücher von Joseph Goebbels*, I/3, 11 June 1938, p. 452.
35. 'Hauptsache ist, dass die Juden hinausgedrückt werden. In zehn Jahren müssen sie aus Deutschland entfernt sein. Aber vorläufig wollen wir die Juden noch als Faustpfand hierbehalten'; ibid. 1/3, p. 490.
36. Ben Elissar, *Diplomatie*, 284 ff.
37. Krausnick, 'Judenverfolgung,' 276. See also Hermann Graml, *Reichskristallnacht, Antisemitismus und Judenverfolgung im Dritten Reich* (Munich, Deutscher Taschenbuch Verlag, 1988).

38. 'Stenographische Niederschrift von einem Teil der Besprechung über die Judenfrage . . .', *TMI* xxviii, PS-1816.
39. Adam, *Judenpolitik*, 217.
40. David Bankier, 'Hitler and the Policy-Making Process on the Jewish Question', *Holocaust and Genocide Studies*, 3/1, 6, convincingly demonstrates Hitler's constant attention to, and multiple interventions in, the anti-Jewish policy of the regime.
41. Adam (*Judenpolitik*, 218–19) speaks of Hitler, apropos this episode, as a 'superior tactician.'
42. Ben Elissar, *Diplomatie*, 383 ff.
43. Avraham Barkai, *Vom Boykott zur 'Entjudung:' Der wirtschaftliche Existenzkampf der Juden im Dritten Reich, 1933–1943* (Frankfurt, Fischer, 1987), 156; Rosenkranz, *Verfolgung*, 227.
44. *ADAP*, D4, doc. 271, p. 293.
45. Lipski to Beck, 20 Sept. 1938, doc. 99. in Jozef Lipski, *Diplomat in Berlin, 1933–1939*, ed. W. Jadrzejewicz (New York, Columbia Univ. Press, 1968), 411.
46. Ben Elissar, *Diplomatie*, 411 ff.
47. *ADAP*, D5, doc. 119, 5 Jan. 1939.
48. *ADAP*, D4, doc. 158, pp. 170–1. 'Die Juden würden bei uns vernichtet. Den 9. November hätten die Juden nicht umsonst gemacht, dieser Tag würde gerächt werden.'
49. *Dokumente der deutschen Politik* (Berlin, Junker & Dünnhaupt, 1940), vii. 476–9.
50. 'Wenn es dem internationalen Finanzjudentum in und ausserhalb Europas gelingen sollte, die Völker noch einmal in einen Weltkrieg zu stürzen, dann wird das Ergebnis nicht die Bolschewisierung der Erde und damit der Sieg des Judentums, sondern die Vernichtung der jüdischen Rasse in Europa sein'; ibid.
51. The great majority of historians report these remarks of Hitler's as if he had linked the extermination to the advent of a war in general. He was speaking of a world war, and he had in mind something other than the European war that would break out a few months later. Let us note that, after the autumn of 1938, certain of his lieutenants spoke of settling accounts with the Jews in the event of war: this is what Goering, in particular, declared on 12 Nov. 1938. Hitler had probably spoken of his intention before his lieutenants: they interpreted it in a vague fashion, but one consistent with the attitude observed at the end of Ch. 1.
52. *TMI*, xxxii, PS-3358; xli, Streicher-8.

3. The Quest for a Territorial Solution, 1939–1941

1. Eugen Kogon, Hermann Langbein, and Adalbert Rückerl, *Les Chambres à gaz secret d'État* (Paris, Minuit, 1984), 24 ff; Ernst Klee, *'Euthanasie' im Dritten Reich* (Frankfurt, Fischer, 1983).
2. *ADAP*, D1, doc. 19, p. 30.

3. Gerhard Eisenblätter, 'Grundlinien der Politik des Reiches gegenüber dem Generalgouvernement, 1939–1945' (diss., Univ. of Frankfurt, 1969), 29–30.

4. See Helmut Krausnick, *Hitlers Einsatzgruppen* (Frankfurt, Fischer, 1985).

5. Martin Gilbert, *Atlas of the Holocaust* (London, Michael Joseph, 1982), 33.

6. BAK, R58/825, 'Amtschefbesprechung am 14.9.39', p. 2; 'Amtschef-und Einsatzgruppenleiterbesprechung', p. 3.

7. 'dass die geplanten Gesamtmassnahmen (also das Endziel) streng geheim zu halten sind', in 'Schnellbrief an die Chefs aller Einsatzgruppen der Sipo,' 21 Sept. 1939, doc. 21, *Faschismus-Getto-Massenmord*, ed. Jewish Historic Institute of Warsaw (Berlin, Rütten & Loening, 1961), 37.

8. Cf. Graml, *Reichskristallnacht*, 192.

9. BAK, R58/825, 'Amtschefbesprechung am 29.9.39'.

10. In a circular dated 30 Sept. and destined for the Einsatzgruppen, he noted the danger that the Jews, once warned, might try to hide; ibid. In the same vein, see Seev Goshen, 'Eichmann und die Nisko-Aktion im Oktober 1939', *VjZ* (Jan. 1981), 81–2.

11. *Das politische Tagebuch Alfred Rosenbergs*, ed. H. G. Seraphim (Munich, Deutscher Taschenbuch Verlag, 1964), 99.

12. 'der Versuch einer Ordnung und Regelung des jüdischen Problems', in *Der grossdeutsche Freiheitskampf: Reden Adolf Hitlers* (Munich, Eher, 1941), i. 95.

13. On 1 Sept. 1939, before the Reichstag; ibid. 26 (and also 35, 99, 126). See also Hitler's speech to the chiefs of staff on 23 Nov. 1939; *Lagevorträge des Oberbefehlshabers der Kriegsmarine vor Hitler 1939–1945*, ed. G. Wagner (Munich, Lehmanns, 1972), 54.

14. *Grossdeutsche Freiheitskampf*, 3 Sept. 1939, i. 35.

15. *Tagebücher von Joseph Goebbels*, I/4, p. 150.

16. *TMI*, xxvi, PS-864.

17. *Staatsmänner und Diplomaten bei Hitler*, ed. A. Hillgruber (Frankfurt, Bernard & Graefe, 1967), doc. 1, p. 30.

18. Krausnick, *Hitlers Einsatzgruppen*, 57.

19. *ADAP*, D8, docs. 419, 477; *Das Diensttagebuch des deutschen General-gouverneurs in Polen, 1939–1943*, ed. W. Prag and W. Jacobmeyer (Stuttgart, Deutsche Verlags-Anstalt, 1975), 82.

20. Goshen, 'Eichmann und die Nisko-Aktion'; Jonny Moser, 'Nisko: The First Experiment in Deportation', *Simon Wiesenthal Center Annual*, 2 (1985), 1–30.

21. *TMI*, xxxvi, EC-305, 'Sitzung über Ostfragen unter dem Vorsitz des Ministerpräsidenten Generalfeldmarschall Göring'.

22. CDJC, clxxxvi-21, 'Endlösung des deutschen Judenproblems'. We already find the expression in a memorandum of 11 Oct. 1939, issued by the chargé for Jewish questions on Bürckel's staff in Vienna; Gerhard Botz, *Wohnungspolitik und Judendeportation in Wien 1938 bis 1945*, Vienna and Salzburg, Geyer, 1975), 105.

23. *Diensttagebuch des deutschen Generalgouverneurs*, 4 Mar. 1940, p. 146.

24. *Faschismus-Getto-Massenmord*, doc. 16, pp. 55–6.

25. *ADAP*, D8, doc. 671, 12 Mar. 1940, p. 716.

26. 'Denkschrift Himmlers über die Behandlung der Fremdvölkischen im Osten (Mai 1940)', *VjZ* (Apr. 1957), 195, 197.

27. Christopher Browning, *The Final Solution and the German Foreign Office* (New York, Holmes & Meier, 1978), 35 ff.

28. Ribbentrop spoke of this to Ciano on 18 June 1940; cf. Galeazzo Ciano, *Diario 1937–1943*, ed. R. de Felice (Milan, Rizzoli, 1980), 443.

29. 'Führer will Madagaskar für Judenunterbringung unter französischer Verantwortung verwenden'; *Lagevorträge*, 107.

30. *Diensttagebuch des deutschen Generalgouverneurs*, 12 July 1940, 252.

31. *Tagebücher von Joseph Goebbels*, I/4, 17 Aug. 1940, p. 284.

32. PA-AA, *Inland IIg*/177, note by Luther, 15 Aug. 1940, 'Mitteilung für Herrn Rademacher'.

33. *Allianz Hitler–Horthy–Mussolini*, ed. L. Kerekes (Budapest, Akademiai Kiado, 1966), doc. 92, p. 287.

34. 'vielleicht aber schon in wenigen Monaten'; CDJC, CLiii-259.

35. *Staatsmänner und Diplomaten bei Hitler*, doc. 46, 20 Nov. 1940, p. 348.

36. A good many historians (notably Philip Friedman, Gerald Reitlinger, and Lucy Dawidowicz) have wanted to see these projects as a cover-up for extermination. Jäckel (*Hitler in History*, 51) believes that there is no indication that Hitler seriously considered the Madagascar project: this assertion is even more difficult to prove than the opposite point of view. I fully endorse Christopher Browning's opinion in 'Nazi Resettlement Policy and the Search for a Solution to the Jewish Question, 1939–1941', *German Studies Review*, 9 (Oct. 1986), 497–519.

37. *Staatsmänner und Diplomaten bei Hitler*, doc. 10, p. 96; see also *Politisches Tagebuch Alfred Rosenbergs*, 120 (27 Jan. 1940).

38. *Tagebücher von Joseph Goebbels*, I/3, 3 Nov. 1939, p. 630; 17 Nov. 1939, p. 645; I/4, 6 Feb. 1940, p. 34.

39. See e.g. the 31 Dec. 1939 message, *Grossdeutsche Freiheitskampf*, i. 132–4; the 19 July 1940 speech, ii. 50; the 4 Sept. 1940 speech, ii. 93.

40. Ibid., 30 Jan. 1940 speech, i. 154; 24 Feb. 1940, i. 166.

41. Ibid., same speeches as above, i. 154, 175.

42. Ibid., 24 Feb. 1949 speech, i. 159.

43. 'das die Juden doch am Ende immer sehr dumm sind', *Tagebücher von Joseph Goebbels*, I/4, p. 127.

44. *Grossdeutsche Freiheitskampf*, ii. 116.

45. 'Die Judengefahr muss von uns gebannt werden. Aber sie wird doch in einigen Generationen wieder auftauchen. Ein Allheilmittel dagegen gibt es gar nicht', *Tagebücher von Joseph Goebbels*, I/3, p. 658.

46. Ibid. I/4284.

47. *Kriegstagebuch des OKW*, ed. P. E. Schramm (Frankfurt, Bernard & Graefe, 1965), i. 257 (9 Jan. 1941). On Hitler's strategy during this period, see Andreas Hillgruber, *Hitlers Strategie, Politik und Kriegführung, 1940–1941* (Frankfurt, Bernard & Graefe, 1965); Saul Friedländer, *Hitler et les États-Unis, 1939–1941* (Paris, Seuil, 1966), English trans. *Prelude to Downfall: Hitler and the US, 1939–1941*

(London, Chatto & Windus, 1967); *Das Deutsche Reich und der Zweite Weltkrieg*, ed. Militärgeschichtliches Forschungsamt, iii, iv (Stuttgart, Deutsche Verlags-Anstalt, 1983, 1984).

48. *Kriegstagebuch des OKW*, i. 275 (21 Jan. 1941).
49. *Grossedeutsche Freiheitskampf*, ii. 222.
50. 'Er dächte über manches jetzt anders, nicht gerade freundlicher', *Heeresadjudant bei Hitler 1938–1943: Die Aufzeichnungen des Majors Engel*, ed. H. von Kotze (Stuttgart, Deutsche Verlags-Anstalt, 1974), 94–5.
51. *Tagebücher von Joseph Goebbels*, I/4, 5 Nov. 1940, p. 387; 18 Mar. 1941, p. 543.
52. *Allianz Hitler–Horthy–Mussolini*, 6, Apr. 1941, doc. 102, p. 305.
53. *Staatsmänner und Diplomaten bei Hitler*, doc. 79, pp. 573–4.
54. Franz Halder, *Kriegstagebuch* (Stuttgart, Kohlhammer, 1963), ii. 77 (26 Aug. 1940); note by Best, 19 Aug. 1940, CDJC, xxiv-1.
55. Adam, *Judenpolitik*, 290.
56. Jacob Toury, 'Die Entstehungsgeschichte des Austreibungsbefehls gegen die Juden der Saarpfalz und Badens', *Jahrbuch des Instituts für deutsche Geschichte*, 15 (1986), 447–50.
57. *Diensttagebuch des deutschen Generalgouverneurs*, 15 Jan. 1941, p. 327.
58. As Lammers wrote to Schirach on 3 Dec. 1940, to communicate this decision, Hitler had decided that this deportation must take place during the war, 'also noch während des Krieges'; *TMI*, xxix, PS-1950. See Botz, *Wohnungspolitik und Judendeportation*.
59. Schellenberg circular, 20 May 1941, NG-3104.
60. CDJC, 'Eichmann Trial', session 77, 22 June, 1961, p. K1.
61. 'Eine Einwanderung von Juden in den von uns besetzten Gebieten ist im Hinblick auf die zweifellos kommende Endlösung der Judenfrage zu verhindern'; cf. n. 59 above.
62. Michael R. Marrus and Robert O. Paxton, *Vichy et les Juifs* (Paris, Calmann-Lévy, 1981), 23; CDJC, V-59, 'Zentrales Judenamt in Paris', 21 Jan. 1941.
63. On 7 June 1941 Lammers wrote to Bormann that Hitler was 'of the opinion that there would no longer be any Jews in Germany after the war' (*Akten der Parteikanzlei*, reconstruction of the originals on microfilm by the Institut für Zeitgeschichte, no. 14695, fo. 101 00437). On 28 Mar. 1941 Rosenberg, speaking of the Jewish reservation that would be created after the war, added that it was 'not necessary to deal at present' with the place of destination: this would be settled later by an international agreement; it mattered little whether it took 'five, ten, or twenty years' to achieve this solution (CDJC, cxlvi-23, 'Die Judenfrage als Weltproblem', p. 67–8).
64. Document reproduced in Helmut Krausnick, 'Hitler und die Morde in Polen', *VjZ* (Apr. 1963), 207.
65. *Tagebücher von Joseph Goebbels*, I/3, 31 Jan. 1939, p. 566.
66. Ibid. I/4, p. 705, 20 June 1941: 'Das Judentum in Polen verkommt allmählich. Eine gerechte Strafe für die Verhetzung der Völker und die Anzettelung des Krieges. Der Führer hat das ja auch den Juden prophezeit.'
67. CDJC, 'Eichmann Trial', session 90, 10 July 1961, p. A1; session 106, 21 July 1961, p. N1.

68. See Christopher Browning, 'Nazi Ghettoization Policy in Poland', *Central European History* (Dec. 1986), 343–68.
69. 'Trials of War Criminals', CDJC, Case 1, 13 May 1947, p. 7484.
70. Brack to Himmler, 28 Mar. 1941, NO-203; Tiefenbacher (Persönlicher Stab RFSS) to Brack, 12 May 1941, NO-204.
71. *From the History of KL Auschwitz*, ed. K. Smolen (Cracow, 1967), i. 2–3.

4. The Fate of the Soviet Jews

1. Testimony of Hermann Gräbe, 'Trials of War Criminals', Case 2 (German transcript), 29 Sept. 1947, p. 45.
2. Besides the works of Krausnick, Reitlinger, Poliakov, etc., already cited, see also Andreas Hillgruber, 'Die "Endlösung" und das deutsche Ostimperium als Kernstück des rassenideologischen Programms des Nationalsozialismus', *VjZ* (Apr. 1972), 133–53.
3. This is notably the position of Billig (*La Solution finale*, 62) and of Browning ('La décision concernant la solution finale', in *L'Allemagne nazie et le Génocide juif*, 197).
4. Alfred Streim is the prosecutor in charge of the Länder's Justice Dept.'s central office for research on Nazi crimes, located in Ludwigsburg (ZStL). For several years he has supported the thesis of an escalation in orders after 22 June; *Die Behandlung sowjetischer Kriegefangener im Fall Barbarossa* (Heidelberg, C. F. Müller, 1981), 74 ff. According to him, however, this escalation was a stratagem by SS leaders to get the operators in the field to intensify their performance of an extermination mission that had been decided at the highest level before the campaign ('Zur Eröffnung des allgemeinen Judenvernichtungsbefehls' gegenüber den Einsatzgruppen' in *Der Mord an den Juden im Zweiten Weltkrieg*, 118).
5. *Kriegstagebuch des OKW*, i. 341 (3 Mar. 1941); Halder, *Kriegstagebuch*, ii. 320 (17 Mar. 1941); ii. 336–7 (30 Mar. 1941).
6. BA-MA, RW 19/185, G. Thomas, 'Aktennotiz über Vortrag beim RM am 26.2.41'.
7. BAK, R70/15.
8. *TMI*, xxvi, PS-502.
9. CDJC, ccxc-10, 'Betrifft: UdSSR', 2 Apr. 1941; the passage concerning the Jews of the Baltic states is found in the 2nd memorandum, 'Betrifft UdSSR, Denkschrift Nr. 2', n.d. (but necessarily after 2 Apr.; the 2 documents were typed on a machine with large characters such as the 'Führermaschine'). A passage from Rosenberg's journal dated 2 Apr. 1941 is often quoted in which, referring to a conversation with Hitler, he noted: 'That which I do not want to put into writing today, but which I will never forget'; quoted by Robert Kempner, *Eichmann und Komplizen* (Zurich, Europa, 1961), 97. I do not know what he had in mind, but, if Hitler had told him of his decision to exterminate the Jews, he would have taken another position in his later writings.
10. 'Allgemeiner Aufbau und Aufgaben einer Dienststelle für die zentrale Bearbeitung der Fragen des osteuropäischen Raumes', 29 Apr. 1941, *TMI*, xxvi, PS-1024. See also Rosenberg to Lohse, 22 July

1941, 'Anweisung an den Reichskommissar des Reichskommissariats Ostland' (CDJC, cxlv-509), where he spoke of putting Jews to work repairing war damage and building roads.

11. 'Die Zivilverwaltung in den besetzten Ostgebieten' ('Braune Mappe'), 'IX. Richtlinien für die Behandlung der Judenfrage', CDJC, ccliv-2, pp. 35–6. Yitzhak Arad ('Alfred Rosenberg and the "Final Solution" in the Occupied Soviet Territories', *Yad Vashem Studies*, 13, 1979, 263–86) also concludes that Rosenberg knew nothing about the extermination of the Jews before the end of the autumn.

12. BAK, NS19/3874, Himmler to Bormann, 25 May 1941, and Bormann to Lammers, 16 June 1941.

13. Dietrich Eicholtz, 'Der"Generalplan Ost" ', *Jahrbuch für Geschichte*, 26 (1982), 256, doc. 2.

14. Wetzel, 24 Apr. 1942, 'Stellungnahme und Gedanken zum Generalplan Ost des Reichsführers SS', reproduced in H. Heiber, 'Der Generalplan Ost', *VjZ* (July 1958), 297–324.

15. On this point I share the opinion of Eisenblätter, ('Grundlinien der Politik des Reiches gegenüber dem General gouvernement', 207 n. 4). His principal arguments are the following: (1) in his covering letter of 15 July 1941 the author, Meyer-Hetling, indicates that the document he drew up was titled *Generalplan Ost*; (2) the June 1942 reformulation makes reference to the 15 July 1941 *Generalplan Ost*; (3) a plan of the same name developed by the RSHA would have been known to Himmler and he would have referred Meyer-Hetling to it; (4) if another *Generalplan Ost* had been drafted at the end of 1941 by the RSHA, the extermination of the Jews would have been taken into account and the Jewish population would not have been included in the total of the populations to be displaced. To which I would add the following arguments: (1) Wetzel indicated having learned in Nov. 1941 that a 'Plan East' had been developed by the RSHA; he did not say the plan had been conceived by the RSHA or conceived at the time he had heard it mentioned; (2) Wetzel even wrote that in this instance the RSHA was clearly acting under orders from the Stabhauptamt des Reichskommissars für die Festigung des deutschen Volkstums, to which Meyer-Hetling specifically belonged; (3) Wetzel was struck by the absence from the list of territories to be colonized of regions such as the Ingermanland, the arc of the Dniepr, the Tauride, and the Crimea; similarly he was struck by a frontier of colonization located this side of the one under consideration at the time he was writing (p. 297). In both cases, the obvious explanation is that the memorandum he was analysing was drafted at a time when Hitler's plans for the various territories to the east were not yet known or finalized, i.e. before the middle of the summer of 1941.

16. Wetzel, 'Stellungnahme', 301.

17. Ibid. 300.

18. *Tagebücher von Joseph Goebbels*, I/4, p. 705.

19. 'in absehbarer Zeit'; *Diensttagebuch des deutschen Generalgouverneurs*, 17 July 1941, p. 386.

20. Ibid. 22 July 1941, p. 389.

21. BAK, R6/21.

22. *ADAP*, D 13, doc. 207, p. 264.

23. Ibid. app. iii, p. 838.
24. 'Trials of War Criminals', Case 9 (German transcript), e.g. p. 641 (14 Oct. 1947); p. 1811 (31 Oct. 1947).
25. Ibid. pp. 316–17 (6 Oct. 1947).
26. Cf. items of judiciary information presented by Alfred Streim in his recent article 'The Tasks of the Einsatzgruppen', *Simon Wiesenthal Center Annual*, 4 (1987), 309–28. Krausnick, for his part, has always defended the thesis of an order given in the spring of 1941 (*Hitlers Einsatzgruppen*).
27. Ohlendorf's defence strategy emerges clearly from his Nuremberg testimony. Having stated that the Führer's order was given before the campaign, he pleaded extenuating circumstances in the form of a superior order that left him no moral choice. Personally, he added, he did not have to pass the order on to anyone, including the leaders of the commando under his authority, since everyone had already been informed about what they had to do (see e.g. 'Trials of War Criminals', Case 9, 14 Oct. 1947, pp. 688–9, 694).
28. The naming of Streckenbach, who was thought to be dead, can probably be explained in the following way: it permitted the avoidance of a surprise in the event of the discovery of a memorandum reporting on Heydrich's remarks during his Berlin speech; it also permitted the safe allegation of the scene of protestation that supposedly followed the transmission of the order.
29. Indictment in the case against Streckenbach, ZStL, 415 AR 1310/63, E 32, ii. 181 ff.
30. Kröger (EK (Einsatzkommando) 3); Ehrlinger (SK (Sonderkommando) 1b).
31. Herrmann (SK 4b), Schulz (EK 5), Nosske (EK 12), Bradfisch (EK 11a). The last 2 had at first said that they had received the order before the campaign.
32. Jäger (EK 3), Blume (EK 7a), Filbert (EK 9), Zapp (EK 11a).
33. Not only was Schulz's version not contested, it was confirmed: thus Blume, leader of EK 7a, who substantiated Ohlendorf's testimony, stated that Heydrich, in his Berlin speech, had 'presupposed' his listeners' knowledge of the Führer's order and therefore had not mentioned it ('Trials of War Criminals', Case 9, 31 Oct. 1947, p. 1817).
34. Ibid. 17 Oct. 1947, 948–9. Same testimony 22 Mar. 1971, ZStL, II 201, AR-Z 76/59, vi. 62.
35. For EK 7a and 9, see *Justiz und NS-Verbrechen* (Amsterdam, Univ. Press Amsterdam, (1966–81), vol. xx, no. 588, pp. 726–7; vol. xviii, no. 540, pp. 616–20; for EK 3, see the Jäger report below.
36. ZStL, II 201 AR-Z 76/59, xi. 7571–2.
37. Ibid. 7578. ZStL, 202 AR-Z 96/1960, p. 3582; *Justiz und NS-Verbrechen*, xviii, no. 540, p. 618.
38. Ibid. xv, no. 465, pp. 52 ff., 194–5.
39. See e.g. ibid. xviii, no. 519, p. 670.
40. 'Trials of War Criminals', Case 9, 8 Oct. 1947, p. 538.
41. ZStL, II 201 AR-Z 76/59, xi. 7608.
42. Ibid. vi. 64–5.
43. Ibid. vii. 35.

44. *Justiz und NS-Verbrechen*, xx, no. 580, p. 436.
45. Cf. Hans-Heinrich Wilhelm, *Die Truppe des Weltanschauungskrieges* (Stuttgart, Deutsche Verlags-Anstalt, 1981), 333 ff.
46. Cf. BAK, R 58/214 ff, *Ereignismeldungen UdSSR (EM)*, no. 13, 5 July 1941 (EG C); no. 14, 6 July 1941 (EG B); no. 22, 14 July 1941 (EG D); no. 27, 19 July 1941 (EG B).
47. *EM* no. 43, 13 July 1941; no. 32, 24 July 1941.
48. 'Einsatzbefehl Nr. 6', 4 July 1941, BAK, R 70 SU/32.
49. *EM* no. 43, 5 Aug. 1941. One must take into account the fact that the dates are those of the RSHA bulletins, and that there may be a time lag with the date of the drafting of the report by the group or the commando. Thus the report already cited figures in another RSHA source, dated 31 July, which means that it must have been drafted during the last week in July ('Tätigkeits-und Lagebericht der EG der SIPO und des SD in der UdSSR', 31 July 1941). We find confirmation of the fact that the Jewish intelligentsia was the priority target in the testimony of an officer/interpreter at Group B headquarters (ZStL, II 201 AR-Z 76/59, ii. 186) and of an administrative head of Commando 10b, group D (ibid. vii. 10).
50. 'um im Sinne einer totalen Vernichtung gegen das hier noch lebende Judentum vorzugehen', *EM* no. 43, 5 Aug. 1941.
51. 'Eine Lösung der Judenfrage während des Krieges. erscheint in diesem Raum undurchführbar, da sie bei der übergrossen Zahl der Juden nur durch Aussiedlung erreicht werden kann', *EM* no. 31, 23 July 1941.
52. 'verwendet und verbraucht', *EM* no. 52, 14 Aug. 1941.
53. *EM* no. 86, 17 Sept. 1941. From an examination of the activity of the EG C during the first months of the campaign, Yaacov Lozowick ('Rollbahn Mord: The Early Activities of Einsatzgruppen C', *Holocaust and Genocide Studies*, 2/2 (1987), 221–41) concludes that there was no extermination order before 22 June.
54. *EM* no. 24, 16 July 1941.
55. BAK, R6/300, 'Protokoll der Besprechung über die politische und wirtschaftliche Lage im Ostland in der Sitzung bei Reichminister Rosenberg am 1. August 1941'.
56. Quoted by Helmut Krausnick, 'Hitler und die Befehle an die Einsatzgruppen in Sommer 1941', in *Der Mord an den Juden im Zweiten Weltkreig*, 101.
57. 'Andererseits hatte die sicherheitspolizeiliche Säuberungsarbeit gemäss den grundstzlichen Befehlen eine möglichst umfassende Beseitigung der Juden zum Ziel' ('Einsatzgruppen A Gesamtbericht bis zum 15. Oktober 1941', 31 Jan. 1942, *TMI*, xxxvii, L-180). Another often-quoted document, drafted by the head of EK 2, Lange, and dating from the beginning of 1942, states that the objective of the commando had been from the beginning 'a radical solution to the Jewish question through the execution of all Jews' (BAK, R70 SU/15). But Lange did not take charge of his commando until Dec. 1941.
58. *EM* no. 19, 11 July 1941.
59. BAK, R 90/146. 'Juden', n.d. (this text refers to Jäger's report of 1 Dec. 1941, quoted below).

60. BAK, R 70 SU/15, Jäger report, 1 Dec. 1941. The totals I present do not include the odd numbers given at the end of the report, which concern executions about which it is unclear whether they occurred in July or Aug.
61. *EM* no. 73, 4 Sept. 1941; no. 108, 9 Oct. 1941; no. 58, 20 Aug. 1941; no. 128, 3 Nov. 1941; no. 89, 20 Sept. 1941; no. 101, 2 Oct. 1941; for the EG A, see the nos. given in Stahlecker's report, *TMI*, xxxvii, L-180.
62. See Yehoshua Büchler, 'Kommandostab Reichsführer SS: Himmler's Personal Murder Brigades in 1941', *Holocaust and Genocide Studies*, 1/1 (1986), 11–25.
63. 'Auf Befehl des HSSPF . . . sind alle als Plünderer überführten männlichen Juden im Alter von 17–45 Jahren sofort standrechlich zu erschiessen', ZStL, CSSR 397.
64. 'Richtlinien für die Durchkämmung und Durchstreifung von Sumpfgebieten durch Reitereinheiten', 28 July 1941, BAK, R70 SU/32.
65. Cf. Krausnick, *Hitlers Einsatzgruppen*, 194; *Justiz und NS-Verbrechen*, xx, no. 570, p. 47.
66. BAK, NS33/22, 'Bericht über den Verlauf der Pripjet-Aktion vom 27.7–11.8.41'.
67. See Mathias Ber, 'Die Entwicklung der Gaswagen beim Mord an den Juden', *VfZ* (July 1987), 403–18.

5. The Final Decision

1. PS-710 (CDJC).
2. Ibid.: 'In Ergänzung der Ihnen bereits mit Erlass vom 24.1.39 übertragenen Aufgabe, die Judenfrage in Form der Auswanderung oder Evakuierung einer den Zeitverhältnissen entsprechend möglichst günstigen Lösung zuzuführen beauftrage ich Sie hiermit, alle erforderlichen Vorbereitungen in organisatorischer, sachlicher und materieller Hinsicht zu treffen für eine Gesamtlösung der Judenfrage im deutschen Einflussgebiet in Europa'.
3. *Ich, Adolf Eichmann*, ed. R. Aschenauer (Leoni am Starnberger See, Druffel, 1980), 479.
4. Luther, 21 Aug. 1942, PA-AA, Inland IIg 177; NG-2596.
5. 'Wenn auch damit zu rechnen ist, dass in Zukunft in den eingegliederten Ostgebieten keine Juden mehr sein werden, halte ich es doch nach den augenblicklichen Verhältnissen für dringend erforderlich, das Standrecht nicht nur für Polen sondern auch für Juden anzuordnen'; *TMI* xxxviii, R-096.
6. 'Im übrigen sei es zu ehrenvoll, die Todesstrafe bei den Juden durch Erschiessen zu vollziehen. Man müsse befehlen, dass sie gehängt würden'; 'Wirtschaftsaufzeichnungen für die Berichtszeit vom 1–14.8.1941 [u. früher]'; Anlage zu: Verb. St. d. OKW/Wi Rü Amt beim Reichsmarschall v. 14.9.41, BA-MA, RW 31/100.
7. CDJC, Eichmann Trial, session 102, 19 July 1961, pp. M1–N1.
8. 'Das Reichsministerium des Innern und die Judengesetzgebung', *VfZ* (July 1961), 297.

9. Dr. Feldscher, 'Ergebnis der Besprechung im Hauptamt Sicherheitspolizei über die Lösung der europäischen Judenfrage', 13.8.1941; Coll. D. Irving, Hitler's War, Microfilm 97125/8 (Microform Academic Publishers; the Institut für Zeitgeschichte has a copy of these documents). When Eichmann, in a letter of 28 Aug. to the Minister of Foreign Affairs, used the phrase 'im Hinblick auf die kommende und in Vorbereitung befindliche Endösung der europäischen Judenfrage', he was referring to this preparatory work.

10. 'Aktenvermerk. Betr. Organisation der Umwandererzentralstelle', Posen, 2 Sept. 1941, with the covering letter of 3 Sept. 1941, to Ehlich (IIIB) and Eichmann (Coll. Irving, Hitler's War, Microfilm 97125/8; it is indicated that the document was obtained by Gerald Fleming from the Polish War Crimes Commission in Warsaw in 1977).

11. The document is reproduced in Adalbert Rückerl, Nationalsozialistische Vernichtungslager im Spiegel deutsche Strafprozesse (Munich, Deutscher Taschenbuch Verlag, 1979), 256–7.

12. Joseph Walk, Das Sonderrecht für die Juden im NS-Staat (Heidelberg, C. F. Müller, 1981), 347.

13. Rosenkranz, Verfolgung und Selbstbehauptung, 269.

14. Justiz und NS-Verbrechen, xxi, no. 591, pp. 125 ff. Cf. Alfred Streim, Sowjetische Gefangene in Hitlers Vernichtungskrieg (Heidelberg, C. F. Müller, 1982).

15. Regarding Auschwitz, some historians, including Hilberg (Destruction des Juifs d'Europe, 763–5), continue to reproduce the testimony of Hoess, the commandant of the camp, who stated that he learned of the extermination order from Himmler in the summer of 1941; Rudolf Hoess, Kommandant in Auschwitz (Munich, Deutscher Taschenbuch Verlag, 1979), 157–8. Everything points to the fact that Hoess was a year out: Himmler would have told him that the existing extermination installations in the east were not capable of expanding operations; shortly afterwards, Eichmann would have described the European method of transporting Jews, the gas trucks used in the east, etc.

16. Goebbels's journal (unedited portion), BAK, NL118/90, 2 Aug. 1941, 17–18.

17. See Lösener's 18 Aug. memorandum, in 'Das Reichministerium des Innern und die Judengesetzgebung', VfZ (July 1961), 302–3.

18. Goebbels's journal, BAK, NL118/90, 19 Aug. 1941, 45 (an error was made in the filming of the journal: the first part of the notes relative to the conversation with Hitler are dated 19 Aug., the remainder 17 Aug.).

19. Lösener memorandum of 18 Aug. 1941, in 'Das Reichministerium des Innern und die Judengesetzgebung', 303.

20. Goebbels's journal, BAK, NL118/90, 19 Aug. 1941 (cf. the remark above), 45; 20 Aug. 1941, 22.

21. Notes written by Rademacher 13 Sept. 1941, quoted by Browning, The Final Solution and the German Foreign Office, 58; cf. also his article 'The Semlin Gas Van and the Final Solution in Serbia', in Fateful Months, 68–85.

22. BAK, NS19/2655.

23. H. G. Adler, Der verwaltete Mensch (Tübingen, Mohr, 1974), 176–7.

24. W. Koeppen notes, 21 Sept. and 7 Oct. 1941, BAK, R6/34a.
25. 'Dies würde aber den Plan einer totalen Aussiedlung der Juden aus den von uns besetzten Gebieten zunichte machen' ('Niederschrift über Besprechung zwischen SS-Obergruppf. Heydrich und Gauleiter Meyer . . . am 4. Oktober 1941', BAK, NS19/1734).
26. Stülpnagel, 6 Oct. 1941, IHTP, H2 646, Mfm A 110.
27. 'Seine Vorschläge wurden von mir erst in dem Augenblick angenommen, als auch von höchster Syelle mit aller Schärfe das Judentum als der verantwortliche Brandstifter in Europa gekennzeichnet wurde, der endgültig in Europa verschwinden muss' (Heydrich to Wagner, 6 Nov. 1941, ibid.).
28. *Das Eichmann Protokoll*, ed. J. von Lang (Frankfurt, Ullstein, 1984), 69. Before the court, Eichmann estimated that the meeting must have taken place in Aug. or Sept. (CDJC, Eichmann Trial, session 92, 11 July 1961, p. Hh1). We can disregard the month of Aug. for the reasons given above.
29. *Eichmann Protokoll*, 69–70. Eichmann probably went to Belzec in Nov. or Dec.; on the other hand, he seemed to remember that the trees were still in leaf. He was also sent to Minsk, but that was during the winter of 1941–2. He also visited Chelmno, where the installation was already functioning, which places his visit after the beginning of Dec. 1941. (CDJC, Eichmann Trial, session 87, 6 July 1961, pp. XI ff.)
30. Cf. e.g. Hilberg, *Destruction des Juifs d'Europe*, 186–8.
31. Übelhör to Himmler, 9 Oct. 1941, BAK, NS19/2655.
32. *Justiz und NS-Verbrechen*, xxi, no. 594, p. 246.
33. *Faschismus-Getto-Massenmord*, doc. 212, p. 278.
34. This is Martin Broszat's thesis: 'Hitler und die Genesis der "Endlösung" ', *VfZ* (Oct. 1977), 739–75; cf. Christopher Browning's response, 'Zur Genesis der "Endlösung": Eine Antwort an Martin Broszat', *VfZ* (Jan. 1981), 97–109.
35. 'Trials of War Criminals', Case 1 (English transcript), 13 May 1947, p. 7504; 19 May 1947, p. 7733.
36. Testimony of Victor Brack, 12 Oct. 1946, NO-426.
37. 'Trials of War Criminals', Case 1 (English transcript), 13 May 1947, pp. 7502–3; 14 May 1947, p. 7514. In his deposition on 13 May 1947, Brack placed his trip to Lublin at 'the beginning of September'; but in the same deposition he mentioned Globocnik speaking to him of his 'special task', and referring to the Jews who were to be deported from the Reich, which excluded the first part of Sept.
38. Testimony of H. B. Gorgass, 23 Feb. 23 1947, NO-3010.
39. The name Globocnik appears frequently in Himmler's agendas: cf. in the *Tagebuch des persönlichen Stabs RFSS* the entries for 9, 15, 17, 20, 25 Oct. (BAK, NS 19/3957); and in Himmler's telephone notes (Telefongespräche) the note on 20 Oct. after a conversation with Daluege: 'collaboration Daluege–Pohl–Globocnik' (NS 19/1438).
40. 'Es sollen die lästigsten Juden herausgesucht werden.'
41. 'Notizen aus der Besprechung an 10.10.41 über die Lösung von Judenfragen', reproduced by H. G. Adler, *Theresienstadt, 1941–1945* (Tübingen, J. C. B. Mohr, 1960), 720–2. I do not take into consideration the remarks contained in Major Engel's entry of 2 Oct. 1941 (*Heeresadjudant bei Hitler*, 111). According to this account,

Himmler gave a report on the deportation of the Jews, then on the situation in the Baltic states and in Ruthenia, and finally on the Jews of Salonika, receiving from Hitler the authorization to deport them. According to the itinerary prepared by his adjutant, Himmler was in the Ukraine on that same 2 Oct. 1941 (BAK, NS19/1792). The reports of Koeppen, Rosenberg's liaison officer with Hitler, mention only the presence of Heydrich on 2 Oct. and refer to Himmler's return from the Ukraine on 5 Oct. (BAK, R 6/43a). The report dates from a later period.

42. BAK, NS19/1438.
43. CDJC, Eichmann Trial, session 98, 17 July 1961, p. Aa1–Bb1; for the date of Himmler's stay in Kiev, See BAK, NS 19/1792.
44. BAK, NS19/1438, entry for 18 Oct. 1941; Müller to Thomas, 23 Oct. 1941, CDJC, xxvi–7.
45. Goebbels's journal, BAK, NL118/91, 24 Sept. 1941, pp. 18–19.
46. Wurm to Rademacher, 23 Oct. 1941, quoted by Browning, *The Final Solution*, 67.
47. Wetzel to Lohse, 25 Oct. 1941, BAK, R90/146.
48. 'Vertraulicher Informationsbericht einer Fahrt durch das General-gouvernment einschliesslich Distrikt Galizien'; Wrocław, 5 Oct. 1941, p. 4. BAK Sammlung Brammer, ZSg 101/41.
49. *Diensttagebuch des deutschen Generalgouverneurs*, 14 Oct. 1941, p. 413.
50. BAK, R6/37.
51. *Diensttagebuch des deutschen Generalgouverneurs*, 16 Dec. 1941, pp. 457–8.
52. CDJC, Eichmann Trial, session 106, 21 July 1961, p. A1; session 107, 24 July 1961, pp. E1, F1.
53. 'Besprechungsprotokoll', CDJC, NG-2586.
54. 29 Sept. 1941, circular from Himmler/Pohl quoted by Olga Wormser-Migot, *Le système concentrationnaire nazi (1933–1945)* (Paris, PUF, 1968), 309–10.

6. Hitler and the Genocide

1. *Kriegstagebuch des OKW*, i (28 May 1941), 412.
2. *Tagebücher von Joseph Goebbels*, I/4, 16 June 1941, p. 695.
3. 'Wir müssen von Anfang an Erfolge haben. Es dürfen keine Rückschläge eintreten'; Halder, *Kriegstagebuch*, ii, 17 Mar. 1941, p. 319; cf. 4 June 1941, p. 443.
4. Hewel's journal, 29 May 1941, Coll. Irving, Hitler's War, Microfilm 97125/4. Hewel, a long-time Nazi, was von Ribbentrop's liaison officer with Hitler.
5. Ibid. 20 June 1941.
6. Ibid.
7. 'Wenn es schief geht, ist sowieso alles verloren'; ibid. 8 June 1941; same idea as 29 May.
8. Ibid. 29 May, 13, 20 June 1941.
9. Ibid. 22 May 1941.
10. Halder, *Kriegstagebuch*, iii, 3 July 1941, p. 38; *Kriegstagebuch des OKW*, i, 4 July 1941, p. 1020.

11. Halder, *Kriegstagebuch*, iii, 8 July 1041, p. 53.
12. Ibid. 10 July 1941, p. 60.
13. 'Das ist der schlimmste Schlag, den ich den Juden versetzt habe'; Hewel's journal, 10 July 1941.
14. Directive no. 32b, 14 July 1941, *Hitlers Weisungen für die Kriegführung, 1939–1945*, ed. Hubatsch (Frankfurt, Bernard-Graefe, 1962), 136–7.
15. *ADAP*, D 13, doc. 50, p. 47.
16. *Lagevorträge*, 9 July 1941, p. 264.
17. *Staatsmänner und Diplomaten*, iii. Dec 83, p. 598–607.
18. Galeazzo Ciano, *Journal politique* (Neuchâtel, La Baconnière, 1947), 50, 53.
19. Cf. Halder's opinion, 23 July 1941, *Kriegstagebuch*, iii. 106.
20. 'Länge des Krieges zehrt an den Nerven'; ibid. 117–18.
21. Quoted by Klaus Reinhardt, *Die Wende vor Moskau: Das Scheitern der Strategie Hitlers im Winter 1941/1942* (Stuttgart, Deutsche Verlags-Anstalt, 1972), 36.
22. Goebbels's journal, BAK, NL118/90, 17 July 1941, p. 5.
23. Ibid. 19 July 1941, p. 5.
24. Ibid. 26 July 1941, p. 12.
25. See Ernst Klink, 'Die Operationsführung: Heer und Kriegsmarine', in *Das Deutsche Reich und der Zweite Weltkrieg*, iv. 489 ff.
26. 'dies geschehe am besten, dass man jeden, der nur schief schaue, totschiesse'; 'Aktenvermerk', *TMI*, xxxviii, L-221.
27. 'Ergänzung zur Weisung 33', *TMI*, xxxiv, C-052.
28. OKH, 25 July 1941, BA-MA, RH 26–221/17. On the army's attitude, see Krausnick, *Hitlers Einsatzgruppen*, 189 ff.; Jürgen Förster, 'Die Sicherung des Lebensraumes', in *Das Deutsche Reich und der Zweite Weltkrieg*, iv. 1033 ff.; Christian Streit, *Keine Kameraden: Die Wehrmacht und die Sowjetischen Kriegsgefangenen 1941–1945* (Stuttgart, Deutsche Verlags-Anstalt, 1978).
29. *ADAP*, D 13, app. III, p. 835–8.
30. *Die Weizsäcker-Papiere 1933–1950*, ed. L. E. Hill (Frankfurt, Propyläen, V 1974), 321 (4 Feb. 1943).
31. Halder, *Kriegstagebuch*, iii. 170, 11 Aug. 1941.
32. 'Die Strategische Lage im Spätsommer 1941 als Grundlage für die weiteren politischen und militärischen Absichten', *ADAP*, D 13/1, doc. 265, p. 346.
33. *Staatsmänner und Diplomaten*, doc. 85, p. 618.
34. Galeazzo Ciano, *L'Europa verso la catastrofe* (Milan, Mondadori, 1948), 670.
35. *Documenti diplomatici italiani*, 9th ser., vol. vii, doc. 512, 26 Aug. 1941, pp. 509, 511.
36. Goebbels's journal, BAK, NL118/90, 19 Aug. 1941, pp. 29–30, 47–8.
37. PA-AA, *Handakten Etzdorf*, 'Zu September 22, 1941'. See also *Weizsäcker-Papiere 1933–1950*, 269 (15 Sept. 1941), 270 (19 Sept.), 271 (28 Sept.); and Goebbels's journal, 24 Sept. 1941, p. 26.
38. *Monologe im Führerhauptquartier 1941–1944*, ed. by W. Jochmann (Munich, Heyne, 1980), 55.
39. 'Sie bewahrheitet sich in diesen Wochen und Monaten mit einer fast unheimlich anmutenden Sicherheit. Im Osten müssen die Juden die Zeche bezahlen: in Deutschland haben sie sie zum Teil schon bezahlt

und werden sie in Zukunft noch mehr bezahlen müssen'; Goebbels
Journal, 24 Sept. 1941, p. 45, 57.

40. *Monologe*, 8 Aug. 1941, p. 57; 17 Sept. 1941, p. 61.
41. Ibid. 59.
42. *Grossdeutsche Freiheitskampf*, iii. 69; 'wenn dieser Krieg länger dauert',
    p. 84.
43. Browning believes, on the contrary, that Hitler reached his major
    decisions regarding the Jews, including the one to kill them,
    during moments when the situation made him 'euphoric' ('Nazi
    Resettlement Policy', 519). It seems impossible to me to describe
    Hitler's emotional states in the summer of 1940 and in the autumn
    of 1941 with the same adjective, 'euphoric'.
44. *Grossdeutsche Freiheitskampf*, iii. 65 (12 Sept. 1941), 65.
45. Ibid., speech for the inauguration of winter relief, 3 Oct. 1941, p.
    74.
46. *Monologe*, 101.
47. Ibid. 107.
48. Halder, *Kriegstagebuch*, iii. 306.
49. Reinhardt, *Die Wende vor Moskau*, 184; cf. also Rolf-Dieter Müller, 'Das
    Scheitern der wirtschaftlichen "Blitzkriegstrategie" ', in *Das Deutsche
    Reich und der Zweite Weltkrieg*, iv. 1022 ff.
50. Goebbels's journal, BAK, NL118/92, 22 Nov. 1941, p. 32.

7. Conclusion

1. See esp. Pierre Vidal-Naquet, *Les assassins de la mémoire* (Paris, La
   Découverte, 1987); *Ist der National-sozialismus Geschichte?*, ed. Dan
   Diner (Frankfurt, Fischer, 1987); Charles S. Maier, *The Unmasterable
   Past: History, Holocaust and German National Identity* (Cambridge:
   Cambridge Univ. Press, 1988).
2. 'From Antisemitism to Extermination', 50.
3. 'Der letzte Entscheid muss ja in dieser Angelegenheit vom Führer
   gefällt werden' ('Trials of War Criminals', Case 1, NO–248.)
4. *Grossdeutsche Freiheitskampf*, iii. 204.
5. Goebbels's journal, BAK, NL118/90, 18 Aug. 1941, p. 12; 26 Aug.
   1941, p. 10.
6. *Diensttagebuch des deutschen Generalgouverneurs*, 16 Dec. 1941, p. 457.
7. Rosenkranz, *Verfolgung und Selbstbehauptung*, 290.
8. Although they differ in every other respect, authors like Nolte and
   Mayer agree on the importance of anti-Bolshevism in the genesis of
   the Final Solution; Ernst Nolte, *Der europäische Bürgerkrieg 1917–1945*
   (Frankfurt, Propyläen, 1987); Arno Mayer, *Why Did the Heavens Not
   Darken?*

Index

Hitler's name has not been included.

ABETZ, Otto, 78, 86
ADAM, Uwe Dietrich, 9, 157, 161
ANTONESCU, Ion, 100, 141
ARAD, Yitzhak, 7, 166

BACH-ZELEWSKI, Erich von dem, 111
BANKIER, David, 161
BECK, Jozef, 61
BILLIG, Joseph, 157, 165
BLOMBERG, Werner von, 41
BLUME, Walter, 169
BORMANN, Martin, 78, 85, 98, 99, 143, 164
BOUHLER, Philippe, 92, 127
BRACK, Victor, 92, 127, 129, 171
BRAUCHITSCH, Walther von, 137
BRÄUTIGAM, Otto, 122
BREITMAN, Richard, 7, 8
BROSZAT, Martin, 9, 159, 171
BROWNING, Christopher, 7, 8, 23, 163, 165, 171, 174
BÜRCKEL, Joseph, 86, 162

CHURCHILL, Winston, 21, 141, 142, 145
CHVALKOVSKY, Frantisek, 61
CIANO, Galeazzo, 137, 163

DAHLERUS, Birger, 71
DAWIDOWICZ, Lucy S., 163
DÉAT, Marcel, 124
DELONCLE, Eugène, 10, 124

EICHMANN, Adolf, 9, 54, 58, 72, 73, 87, 90, 116, 117, 118, 119, 121, 122, 125, 126, 128, 129, 130, 152, 170, 171
EICKE, Theodor, 120
EISENBLÄTTER, Gerhard, 166
ENGEL, Gerhard, 85, 171

FILBERT, Alfred, 103
FLEMING, Gerald, 8, 170
FRANCO, Francisco, 83
FRANK, Hans, 72, 73, 74, 75, 76, 77, 86, 90, 99, 100, 130, 152
FRANKFURTER, David, 52
FRICK, Wilhelm, 42, 47
FRIEDLÄNDER, Saul, 149, 157
FRIEDMANN, Philip, 163

GLOBOCNIK, Odilo, 125, 127, 171
GOEBBELS, Joseph, 38, 42, 43, 46, 47, 50, 51, 52, 55, 57, 59, 60, 70, 77, 80, 81, 85, 89, 90, 99, 120, 121, 129, 130, 134, 137, 142, 143, 146, 150, 152
GOERING, Hermann, 9, 13, 14, 54, 55, 57, 58, 59, 60, 73, 74, 86, 87, 89, 96, 98, 115, 116, 117, 118, 121, 150, 161
GREISER, Arthur, 90, 122, 123, 126, 127, 128, 149
GROSS, Walter, 3, 11, 48, 49, 50, 63
GRYNSZPAN, Hirsch, 57
GUSTLOFF, Wilhelm, 52, 53

HALDER, Franz, 134, 137, 138, 140, 146, 173
HESS, Rudolf, 42, 52
HEWEL, Walter, 172
HEYDRICH, Reinhard, 4, 5, 7, 9, 10, 11, 14, 46, 58, 59, 67, 68, 69, 71, 74, 77, 88, 89, 90, 95, 96, 97, 98, 101, 102, 103, 105, 106, 109, 110, 111, 112, 115, 116, 118, 120, 121, 122, 123, 124, 125, 127, 128, 129, 130, 145, 150, 167, 172
HILBERG, Raul, 156, 157, 170
HIMMLER, Heinrich, 7, 20, 42, 45, 57, 65, 67, 68, 69, 73, 74, 75, 76, 77, 87, 89, 90, 92, 94, 95, 96, 98, 99, 101, 103, 104, 105, 110, 111, 112, 113, 115, 120, 122, 123, 126, 127, 128, 129, 130, 133, 143, 145, 149, 150, 166, 170, 171, 172
HINDENBURG, Paul von, 41, 44
HOESS, Rudolf, 170
HÖPPNER, Rolf-Heinz, 118, 119

JÄCKEL, Eberhard, 9, 22, 158, 161, 165
JÄGER, Karl, 6, 109, 110

KEITEL, Wilhelm, 71, 77, 85, 137, 140, 141
KLEMPERER, Victor, 32
KNOCHEN, Helmut, 124
KOCH, Robert, 136
KOEPPEN, Werner, 172
KRAUSNICK, Helmut, 4, 167
KVATERNIK, Sladko, 139

LAMMERS, Hans, 99, 100, 164
LANGE, Herbert, 126
LANGE, Rudolf, 168
LAVAL, Pierre, 124
LEY, Robert, 85
LIPSKI, Jozef, 60
LOHSE, Heinrich, 108, 129
LOZOWICK, Yaacov, 155, 168

MAYER, Arno, 9, 23, 155, 174
MEYER, Alfred, 123

MEYER-HETLING, Konrad, 166
MOLOTOV, Vyacheslav, 83
MOMMSEN, Hans, 9
MÜLLER, Heinrich, 130
MUSSOLINI, Benito, 83, 86, 136, 137, 142

NAPOLEON, 139
NEBE, Arthur, 112
NEURATH, Constantin von, 41, 44
NOLTE, Ernst, 13, 174
NOSSKE, Gustav, 105
NOVAK, Franz, 152

OHLENDORF, Otto, 5, 101, 102, 104, 105, 169
OSHIMA, Hiroshi, 136

PIROW, Oswald, 60, 61
POLIAKOV, Léon, 157

RAEDER, Erich, 77, 82
RASCH, Otto, 101, 105, 107
RAUSCHNING, Hermann, 33, 160
REITLINGER, Gerald, 163
RIBBENTROP, Joachim von, 41, 56, 77, 83, 141, 163, 172
ROOSEVELT, Franklin D., 14, 21, 61, 83, 141
ROSENBERG, Alfred, 10, 62, 68, 69, 78, 98, 99, 108, 122, 123, 129, 130, 164, 165, 167, 172
ROSS, Colin, 75

SCHACHT, Hjalmar, 42, 47, 48, 55, 59
SCHIRACH, Baldur von, 164
SCHLEUNES, Karl A., 155, 160
SCHMUNDT, Rudolf, 122
SCHULENBURG, Friedrich Werner von der, 140
SCHULZ, Erwin, 101, 102, 104, 105, 167
SPEER, Albert, 85
STAHLECKER, Walther, 101, 103, 108
STALIN, Joseph, 79, 82, 83, 134, 138, 139, 142

STRECKENBACH, Bruno, 5, 101, 102, 167

STREICHER, Julius, 42, 43, 46, 47, 48, 129

STREIM, Alfred, 4, 155, 165, 167

STÜLPNAGEL, Otto von, 10, 124

TODT, Fritz, 146

ÜBELHÖR, Friedrich, 11, 125, 126

WAGNER, Robert, 86

WETZEL, Erhard, 166

WIRTH, Christian, 127